The Whole Story

The National Writing Project publishes books for teachers to support its primary goal to improve student writing and learning by improving the teaching of writing in the nation's schools. Other books from the National Writing Project include:

Teachers at the Center: A Memoir of the Early Years of the National Writing Project. By James Gray.
Teacher-Researchers at Work. By Marion S. MacLean and Marian M. Mohr.
The Writer's Workout Book: 113 Stretches Toward Better Prose. By Art Peterson.
A Poem for Every Student: Creating Community in a Public School Classroom. By Sheryl Lain.
Cityscapes: Eight Views from the Urban Classroom. By members of the NWP Urban Sites Network.
I Can Write What's on My Mind: Theresa Finds Her Voice. By Sherry Seale Swain.
Writing Your Heritage: A Sequence of Thinking, Reading, and Writing Assignments. By Deborah Dixon.

Please direct reprint requests and book orders to:

National Writing Project
2105 Bancroft Way #1042
Berkeley, California 94720-1042
www.writingproject.org

The Whole Story

TEACHERS TALK ABOUT PORTFOLIOS

Edited by
Mary Ann Smith
and Jane Juska

NATIONAL WRITING PROJECT
Berkeley, California

National Writing Project, Berkeley 94720

Design and composition: Seventeenth Street Studios

Library of Congress Cataloging-in-Publication Data

The whole story: teachers talk about portfolios / edited by Mary Ann
Smith and Jane Juska.
    p. cm.
Includes bibliographical references.
ISBN 1-883920-17-5 (pbk.)
1. Portfolios in education. 2. English language—Composition and exer-
cises—Study and teaching. I. Smith, Mary Ann, 1942- II. Juska, Jane.
LB1029.P67 W56 2001
371.3—dc21
                                               2001044568

*We cannot get a valid picture of a
student's writing skill unless we look
at more than one sample produced on
more than one day in more than
one mode or genre....*

—Peter Elbow,
*Embracing Contraries:
Explorations in Learning and Teaching*

Contents

Introduction

Mary Ann Smith

Too much of school life is about preparing for another life—for the sixth grade if you're in fifth grade, for college if you're in high school. Too many students, particularly in recent years, prepare for their next life by enduring the most narrow curriculum imaginable, one focused solely on readying them for a large-scale, standardized test. Increasingly, growing up in school means getting into shape for the next onslaught.

Portfolios, too, are about coming of age but by an entirely different means. In fact, portfolios capture growth itself by featuring a selection of student work—work that students accumulate and revise over time. In doing so, portfolios invite students to care about their growth.

Several years ago, I witnessed an event that showed me the extent of that care. I hadn't been to a school assembly of students since my own school days, and I'd been told that assemblies at Mt. Diablo High School in Concord, California, were dicey affairs. The question was what kind of boisterous entertainment would captivate the students who, admittedly, had a habit of wandering away. Surely, the least attractive program would be one about school itself, about academic achievement. Yet the Mt. Diablo English teachers managed to corral their students into the multipurpose room for an end-of-the-year gathering to celebrate their writing portfolios.

These particular English teachers had already taken much bigger chances than organizing a mere assembly of students. Four years prior to this gathering, they had greeted the school's incoming ninth-graders with a portfolio project that would consume a fair share of the energy students are willing to invest in high school. Together the teachers and students had hammered out what the portfolio should contain. Each year thereafter, members of the English department read the portfolios in May, writing letters of support, critique, and next steps for each student.

Now the ninth-graders had become graduating seniors. If they had truly embraced the idea of portfolios, they might give the assembly a chance. There was food, after all. The school's restaurant program catered the event. There was a graduation-like ceremony during which students were to receive a real record of their four years of high school—portfolios of their work. The English department—all ten members—marched up the aisle of the assembly hall in preparation for the ceremony. Instantly, the students leaped up and applauded with the raucous excitement traditionally reserved for football coaches. Was this a case of mistaken identity? And from the students' point of view, what elevated this gathering to a pep rally?

In fact, the students' enthusiasm for their teachers and the project they grew together is one of the themes of this book. The Mt. Diablo story illustrates that portfolios are often a cause for celebration. Students actually relish the idea of selecting and presenting their work and of coming to terms with its quality. They are willing accomplices in overturning the traditional hierarchy, which gives teachers—and more recently, policymakers—all the say-so in charting progress and setting goals. What's more, students are more likely to take care of what belongs to them—in this case, their portfolios—just as owners take more care of their surroundings than renters.

Portfolios as Sources of Pride

Several of the Mt. Diablo students described their portfolios as "scrapbooks of my life" because they contain memories right along with evidence of achievement. Rather than whittling a student down to a peg-in-a-hole test score, portfolios portray the student from many angles and time periods. Two of the chapters in this book highlight the fact that when portfolios are stocked with student-selected pieces, they also serve as historical markers of a student's journey.

In her chapter, "Throw Me a Life Jacket: The Portfolio as an Instrument of School Survival," Lisa Piazza describes her students as they dig through their portfolios at the end of a school year, coming across "old friends; parts of themselves they had long since forgotten." For Jane Juska's students in "What We Write About When We Write About Love," the portfolio "belongs to them as nothing else can. . . . " These students happen to be adult prisoners in San Quentin State Prison.

Portfolios as Evaluation

In the best circumstances, portfolios represent a student's individual growth and accomplishments to date. They chronicle movement. Where end-of-unit or end-of-year tests are like stop-action photos—with their subjects too often caught off guard—portfolios offer a series of shots. Thus, they assess student learning more fairly.

Compare a test that asks students to make instant decisions to one that asks them to engage in all the complexities of being a writer or a mathematician or a scientist. In the former circumstance, students identify answers—someone else's answers—whose currency is limited to the questions at hand. In the latter, their "answers" are actual performances that demonstrate some requirement or standard of the discipline.

Can we surmise, then, that students will meet a higher standard, even write more effectively, in a portfolio environment? In his chapter, "Breaking the Rules," David Wood contrasts the quality of writing on final exams—"essays written on the same or similar topics about which few of the students care, under circumstances that promote bad thinking and writing"—with "some downright spectacular" writing that shows up in student portfolios.

Unlike tests that are the lucrative stone tablets of a publishing or testing company or that purport, in their multiple-choice formats, to represent standards, portfolios can be dynamic and open-ended. Students and teachers can negotiate the contents of the portfolio so that students fulfill requirements yet still have the chance to show off what they consider their best efforts. John Dorroh in "The Evolution of a Biology Teacher" describes how he and his students invented a whole lineup of performances in science that could become part of their evaluation portfolios.

Moreover, portfolio evaluation is closer to real-life evaluation than are standardized tests, dropped off at the classroom door from some distant outpost. With portfolios, students have support to rethink and revise their work before subjecting it to scrutiny. They have the chance to explain what they've done, put it in a context or framework, with the reflective letters or notes they write as accompaniment. And students may expect more than one person to examine their work, including peers, family members, neighbors, other teachers, administrators, and, of course, the students themselves. Three authors—Patricia McGonegal, Mary Kay Deen, and Sherry Swain—devote parts of their chapters to the ways they bring parents into the portfolio assessment process.

Portfolios as a Teaching and Learning Tool

Portfolios extend the time devoted to writing and revising rather than collapsing the time, as other assessments do. Teachers, like those we meet here, invite students to revisit their work and give it another shot, perhaps applying new strategies they've learned to "old" pieces. For Judith Ruhana's middle school students, the quarterly selection of pieces for their portfolios is coupled with a week for revision so students are "more in control of their grades and their own growth." Similarly, Patricia McGonegal uses a series of approaches to teaching writing, creating with her students a portfolio culture that honors both processes and products.

Equally important, assembling portfolios requires students to judge which pieces of writing are more worthy or satisfying than others and why. Often they have to choose one piece over another or select a piece that fits into a particular category, for example, a persuasive paper. To make these kinds of decisions, students have to apply criteria. For Sherry Swain in "How Portfolios Empower Process Teaching and Learning," her first-graders use "their internalized sense of what makes good writing," which becomes more sophisticated over time.

Portfolios involve students in an adult enterprise. In an era when many teachers are required to devote one or more days a week to the mechanics of test prep, portfolios preview real-world tasks. Joni Chancer in "The Teacher's Role in Portfolio Assessment" explains how she gives her fourth and fifth grade students models of how adults read and write. To introduce the notion of portfolios, for example, she starts "by discussing various professionals who use portfolios in real-life situations . . . architects, advertising consultants, artists, and even fashion models." In another chapter, "Writing History: Portfolios, Student Perspective, and Historical Understanding," Stan Pesick chronicles what happens when his students are no longer able to count on "the trusty end-of-chapter questions as a way of completing history assignments" or on "encyclopedia rearranged" writing. To come closer to an adult standard of historical thinking, his students compile portfolios in which they refine and revise their views of history.

Portfolios as a Tool for Reform

Nine years ago, the National Writing Project (NWP) published a book called *Teachers' Voices: Portfolios in the Classroom*. Teachers wrote about how they designed portfolios that put a premium on students' needs, on serious, innovative curricula, and on classroom cultures that supported rather than sabotaged excellent writing. They gave buoyant, optimistic descriptions and displays of how student performances improved. At the same time, they warned readers not to make portfolios the next magic bullet; indeed, they urged that portfolios be protected from the kind of blind mimicry that often kills invention in education.

This book, intended to show in what ways portfolio practices may have changed, has a noticeably different theme from its predecessor. While once again, teachers make their cases for portfolios, they do so in a policy environment skewed toward standardized, external assessments, which claim—in their annual appearances—to mirror high standards and nab those who haven't met them. Hence, teachers are compelled to argue for principles they once may have taken for granted. In her chapter "Bellringers," for example, Mary Kay Deen insists that the voices and ideas of students still count, that they must not be crushed by the mill of grades and tests and master time lines that ignore an individual's growth and development.

On the other hand, the current climate—the increasing demands that teachers teach only approved approaches from approved textbooks or programs—is infectious. Even well-meaning teachers can fall prey to bureaucratic thinking and, ironically, impose it on their colleagues. In her chapter "The Birth and Death of Portfolio Assessment 1992–2000," Pauline Sahakian describes the way a group of veteran teachers in her high school "handed down" their portfolio system to incoming teachers, asking the newcomers to simply follow the established procedures for the already-approved portfolio program. Stripped of their professionalism, the teachers for whom portfolios were a mandate from above gave them only lip service and, ultimately, a merciful burial.

At this point, the issue is the extent to which portfolios are worth supporting as a viable tool for reform, particularly with regard to writing and learning. Current legal tender, whether a mandated exam or a packaged program, hardly seems to include portfolios. Yet when teachers are limited to what's on the page—printed instructions, checklists, or procedures—they often avoid teaching writing because they may lack strategies for doing so. If anything, the activities that make up a portfolio culture are crucial to teaching and learning: reading and writing with students, creating rubrics, using models, conducting conferences, working through multifaceted revision and editing strategies, practicing reflection and analysis, and responding to student work.

Along with specific teaching strategies, teachers need firsthand experiences with how to use these strategies and why they are important. Through the National Writing Project, all of the teachers represented in this book have had a professional community of colleagues to rely on as they have developed their portfolio programs. A hallmark of this community has been its recognition that informed teachers are the key to improving student learning. Rather than falling on a sword for one approach to literacy, the project has promoted through its teacher-leaders a vast repertoire of practices. For unless teachers have the means to teach the complex processes and demands of writing—developing ideas, shaping arguments, drawing conclusions, to name a few—they are unlikely to make a dent in student writing perform-ances. And unless they have a flexible set of practices to serve an increasingly diverse student population, they are unlikely to reach every child.

The NWP teachers represented in this book employ a wealth of teaching strategies in order to teach with portfolios. In fact, the ethic related to portfolios is one of enlarging the curriculum, the opportuni-ties to write, and the support for young writers. If our goal in educa-tion is to increase the capacities of teachers and students—to expand their options, their knowledge, and their resourcefulness—then port-folios should be high on the list of practices.

How Portfolios Empower Process Teaching and Learning

Sherry Seale Swain

A Mississippi teacher notes how her first-graders become more and more sophisticated in writing portfolio reflections on what they have learned.

ather all your writing, all the things that are in your writing folder or posted on the wall, anything you have published or that you are still working on. Spread it before you. Now try to choose one piece that shows you are a good writer."

It's portfolio selection day, and my first-graders recognize these instructions as one of the learning processes of our classroom. A passion for observing developing literacy led me to design a portfolio project to reveal growth in reading and writing over time, so four times during the year my students collect all their writing, published and in-process, and choose one as their best piece. (Four similar selections from their reading workshop journal entries show that they are becoming better readers, but for this article I will confine my story to what happens with the writing only.)

After the students write reflective pieces explaining what their selections show about their writing abilities, the written reflections are attached to copies of the selected pieces of writing and placed in the students' portfolios. The portfolios are thinner, neater than writing folders and insure student awareness and ownership of learning. More on that later.

Selecting

Selecting pieces for the portfolios requires time for talking and sorting and explaining and responding to preferences. Usually, most of my students have five or six items to choose from, although some have only two or three. If you were to walk into the classroom during this process, you'd notice most of the children standing somewhere near their desks, sharing piles of work with friends.

"Look, I have five: two fact, two fiction, and one riddle book. Are riddles fact or fiction?"

"Hey, we both made pop-up books. Mine is like Eric Carle's."

"That's funny when you made him say, 'In your face!'"

"Help me decide. I like my research book, but my group likes my personal narrative."

Criteria for selections are never posted on a chart or directed with predetermined questions. They emerge from a student's internalized sense of what makes good writing. Kelly says, "I chose my *Cotton* book because I like the way I used a narrator in it, sort of like *The Big Hungry Bear and the Red Ripe Strawberry*. But really I have a double narrator. One asks questions and the other one answers them."

Bonn grins, "I tried to use interesting words in this one like *appeared* and *tumbled*, and *scrambled*, and *crawled*."

I follow up by inviting others to learn from Kelly and Bonn, "Did anyone else choose a book with a narrator? A book with interesting words?" What one student expresses gives clues to what others are ready to learn. After listening to Bonn talk about interesting words, Roger re-examines his selection, a book that has resulted from his animal research on snakes. He revises again (although the book was published days ago), adding words and phrases he thinks are interesting: *coiled up like a ball and a crayola* and *poisoned*. All I have to do is spotlight individual learning and incite others to enter into it. Those who are ready, do. Those who are not ready for one concept pick up another. Samantha selects a draft that contains pages describing what she likes about school and several pages about going camping. She doesn't connect with Kelly's and Bonn's criteria, but when she hears Daniel say that his book is about just one thing, she begins to sort her pages into two separate books. She has the criteria she needs for now; there will be many more opportunities for focusing on narrators and vivid verbs.

Whatever their criteria at a given time, the selection process takes the students back into their writing. Murphy and Smith (1991) contended that the selection process forces students to distance themselves from the piece, to view it as an artifact, a symbol that represents who they are as writers on that day, in that moment of their growth. Selecting becomes part of the learning process.

Reflection

Reflecting on the selections also requires time, but, without it, we have no portfolio, just a collection of writing. "Look carefully at your choice," I advise. "Think about all the reasons you chose it." Sometimes partners orally share and explain how the chosen pieces show they are good writers. Sometimes we sit cross-legged in a circle on the rug, each person revealing his or her selection and the values attached to it. Mary Beth shares a green poster of an ocean scene with a four-line sentence written in her unique style across the top. On the left side of the poster are photographs and small bits of paper secured by single pieces of tape. She lifts the bits of paper, showing more text underneath. "I picked this one because it shows I can make a double peek-a-boo." The circle disintegrates as her classmates crawl across the rug for a better look.

"How did you do that?"

"Hey, I'm gonna try that in my next book. I bet I can make three peek-a-boos!"

Back at their desks, selected pieces before them, students write their reflections. "At the top of your paper, write the word *Reflections*," I say, writing it on a chart paper for them to copy. "Then write to explain to yourself, to your classmates, to me, and to other teachers who may want to read your portfolio, how your selection shows that you are a good writer. Remember all the reasons you chose it. Remember everything your friends said about it. Remember what you said to your partner or in the circle." I encourage volume as they write the reflections because I believe that writing is generative, that the more you write the more you discover and understand what you know. I am quite willing to read the same thoughts expressed over and over as students struggle for an insight that can come only after much milling of the obvious. When some students seem to have run out of steam , I usually say, "Now turn through your book, page by page. Write about all the wonderful things you did in it."

Like I said, I go for volume. But I don't always get it. Nor do my students always write what I consider to be quality reflections. In October for the first selection/reflection process, twelve of the seventeen students who wrote reflections selected pieces because they valued the mechanics of their handwriting! I was crushed. I had not emphasized letter formation or even neatness. My students had learned to draw letters of the alphabet out of a need to write poems, stories, thoughts. Not once had we practiced making line after line of balls and sticks. I consoled myself with the thought that, as a baseline, at least these reflections were guaranteed to reveal growth in the end!

For her first selection, Jennifer chose a poster she'd made in response to my reading of *Ramona the Brave* by Beverly Cleary. Daniel chose a book he'd made as a result of our cotton study. Their reflections are shown here:

JENNIFER

Poster based on *Ramona the Brave*

I picked this because we read Ramona. Ramona had to go to the front of the room. It was my best handwriting.

DANIEL

Cotton

I picked this because I put question marks and I put flaps.

[Daniel had written additional text under each of his "flaps."]

It was January before we selected pieces of writing again. While most of the October responses had been one or two sentences in length, these were longer, ranging from a half to a full page. This time only three of the fifteen students who wrote reflections mentioned mechanics. Nine talked about the content of their pieces; eight referred to their writing process; nine pointed out elements of style; one called attention to response from another class member; and one referred to illustration. Jennifer and Daniel's responses read:

JENNIFER

Jennifer's Family

This shows I am a good writer because it is my best book. I like the book because I like when my baby doll said, "This is fun." I like my characters. They are a baby doll, a gray dog, a dad, a mom.

DANIEL

The Monsters in My Dreams

I picked this because it is a long book. I put who the characters are. I wrote all about one thing, and kept on adding words until it was just right.

By March when we wrote the third reflections, many of the twenty-one responding students filled a notebook page with thoughts about their writing. Fifteen reflected on elements of style they had learned; fifteen recognized the value of their content; ten called attention to their writing processes; six wrote about revising. One student mentioned response from another class member, and one referred to illustration. Jennifer, having made revisions to it, chose *Jennifer's Family* again while

Daniel chose a wordless book by Ezra Jack Keats to which he and his friend Bonn had added text. Jennifer and Daniel were the only two students who mentioned mechanics in their reflections.

JENNIFER

Jennifer's Family

This book shows I am a good writer because I put talking on the first page and on the last page. I put periods on every page. I put people's names on pages 2, 3, 4. I put funny stuff on pages 4, 5, 6. I went back and added other words on pages 2 and 6. My book is about my family. I picked this book because my family is the best.

DANIEL

Skates

This book shows I am a good writer because I wrote action. Look on pages 1, 3, 4, 5, 6, 8, 9, 10, 11, and 13 where I put action in. I put commas, conversation bubbles, apostrophes, and quotation marks. I made long sentences. I filled the page. I put crashing words on pages 3, 5, 7, and 14. I changed some words that I didn't like. I put words that the dogs said when they got hurt on pages 5, 9, and 11. I named the dogs weird names.

And I wrote a lot on this paper that shows I am a good writer.

By May none of the twenty-four students who participated in the selection/reflection process mentioned mechanics. Seventeen called attention to style, thirteen to content and process; eight described response; six discussed revision; and six commented on illustration. Jennifer selected a personal narrative about her struggle to learn to feed her family's fish. Daniel chose a lengthy piece of fiction that had been through numerous revisions.

JENNIFER

Fishyfoo

This book shows I am a good writer because it was about when I was young. What did you like about my book? I put talking. I put names of people. I put pictures. I put a big word. It was just **popped** in the kitchen. *Jamie helped me figure out to put in* Just when Kelley left *instead of just putting* My sister spent a night with Mandy. I fed too much food, then they died that night. *Then I put that just after (the word)* Mandy. *I put* Just when Kelley left. *I put a picture on the first page. The name of this book is* Fishyfoo. [Jennifer's original sentences read: *My sister spended a night with Mandy. I fed too much food, then they died that night.* Her revision reads: *My sister spended a night with Mandy. Just when Kelley left, I fed too much food, then they died that night.*]

DANIEL

Secrets of the Ninja

I think this is my best book because I used dialect. I used a bigger binder than I did in any of my books. I worked on it for a long time. I put a lot of words. I was careful with my pictures. I made four pages without any words and I decided to stop drawing pictures until I got more words in. I named all my characters, even me. I used interesting words. I did a dedication page. I colored my pictures. I spelled my name, my mom's name and my dad's name backwards for some monsters' names. I tried to model a page sounding like one in Charlotte's Web.

Criteria

Each time students chose pieces for their portfolios, their personal selection criteria seemed to become more sophisticated, and I was sure that the increased fluency of their reflections represented internalized appreciation for their growth as writers. The portfolios were an empowering writing process for my students! I made sure the classroom procedures allowed them to be aware of each other's criteria before, during, and after the selection process. The environment was rich with opportunities, expectations even, to learn from each other. The notion of learning in a portfolio classroom is not a foggy, nebulous concept. Learning is concrete, and portfolios offer concrete evidence. Jennifer's and Daniel's reflections show a typical increase in fluency and increasing sophistication. The chart in Figure 1 shows a progression of the entire class. (The variations in the numbers of students responding are due to students transferring in and out of the class, a long illness, and ESL students becoming more fluent in English.)

FIGURE 1

COMPONENTS OF REFLECTIONS	OCTOBER REFLECTIONS	JANUARY REFLECTIONS	MARCH REFLECTIONS	MAY REFLECTIONS
	(17 students)	(15 students)	(21 students)	(24 students)
Mechanics	12	3	2	0
Content	1	9	15	13
Process	3	8	10	13
Revision	0	0	6	6
Response	1	1	1	8
Illustration	1	1	1	6
Style	2	9	15	17

Portfolios close the gap often left open when we follow the maxim: children learn by doing. They do, but the doing itself is not the key. To paraphrase John Dewey (1916), we must have our students involved in not only the doing, they must also observe themselves in the doing, and reflect on their observations. In a writing-based classroom, the doing is writing, observing, drawing, moving, experimenting, manipulating, dramatizing, reading, rewriting, seeking response to writing, revising, rethinking, adding to, taking out, writing for oneself, writing for publication, writing for the joy of seeing words dance across the page, writing.

In a writing community, students talk and write to observe themselves as writers. They talk about their writing in whole-class sharing circles and in intimate response groups. Frequently during our writing workshops, a writer will ask a group of two to four students to gather on the rug to respond to his or her draft. They sit in tight circles, eyes intent on the writer, as she reads. "What do you like about my book?" she'll ask, expecting a detailed answer from each responder. And detailed answers flow. My students have learned from experience that general compliments (I like your whole book) are not helpful to the writer. Sometimes the responders want a closer look at certain pages; sometimes they ask to hear the book again; often they break off into a discussion of how the writer's book reminds them of a personal experience or of another book. They notice when a friend has worked out a complicated plot. They notice elements of style and compliment effective use of dialogue and metaphor. Then the writer asks, "What would make my book better?" Her responders again make specific comments that lead to improvements:

"I don't understand the part about the talking mermaid doll gift. On the other page, it sounded like you already had one."

"Shouldn't the page about coming down the stairs go before the page about opening presents?"

"You could write a dedication page to your dad since the story is about him."

In my class, students also come every few days for writing conferences with me. "What have you done so far?" I ask, and Daniel describes his process of illustrating about four pages at a time, then writing text for those before proceeding. Then he reads his draft, and I compliment the complex plot he has begun. "Have you tried anything new in this piece?" I ask, and he explains the dialect he has written for one of the characters. He is especially proud of a page he has modeled after one in *Charlotte's Web*. We celebrate briefly by sharing it with the rest of the class. Daniel's book is wonderful, but I have some honest questions about the content. "Help me understand how the crystal ball fits into the story," I say. "I don't understand how it suddenly appeared." Daniel explains the significance of the ball and tells how he will infuse that information into his book. "What do you need to do next?" I ask to help him set goals at the end of the conference. Later when Daniel chooses this book for his portfolio, he cements his observations in writing.

I've described a hefty investment of instructional time for talking and writing about learning. Observing themselves as writers is important to students' awareness of their own learning; we need to allow time for it.

Walls Come Down

We've already talked about reflection, the clasping link in the learning chain. It falls into the category of "worth it in the long run." However, there are walls, tall and thick, to push through at different times during the year. You have to push through their gloom sometimes with nothing more than faith that there is a brighter light on the other side. One of those first walls for me was the initial selection time, because I didn't feel the children knew enough and I couldn't teach or model enough to let them internalize valid criteria before that first selection. I was disappointed that so many valued their handwriting. And I felt guilty. Somehow I must have been responsible for those attitudes. Reflection (my own), though, reassured me that their baseline criteria would let me see real growth in their thinking later in the year.

That wall was thick, and its weight bore heavily for weeks—but the light on the other side was there all the time. The October reflections compared to March and May reflections illuminate growth in every single student! What's more, I now realize that handwriting was important in October because, for many students, letter formation represented their newest learning. As forming letters became more commonplace, handwriting retreated to its proper position—a mere tool.

The children themselves erected the second wall when I announced that it was time for the January selections. "Aww," they groaned, "we'd rather write in our writing folders." How disappointing it was to see them not value their own portfolios. Faith again helped us all through that wall, and perhaps it was the most important one of all. For shortly after that second selection and reflection process, I began to see signs of real internalization and consciousness of their own growth in reading and writing. In our sharing circle, students began to call attention to their strengths, prefacing their comments with, "Did you notice that I told what the book reminded me of?" or "I started to use the word *ran* here but changed it to *raced*." I also received a note from Mary Beth's mother explaining that Mary Beth had been making her parents aware of her own language growth: "Mama, did you hear me say 'a sea of trees'? That's better than just saying 'a forest.'"

Meta-reflection

Now let's look at the dimension that's added when students engage in meta-reflection, when they reflect on reflections. Picture the writing portfolio after students have selected and reflected several times. Copies of each selection are stacked in a chronological order in the pocket of a folder. Attached to each selected piece of writing is the written reflection the student made at the time of the selection. Most of my students had four such pieces in May when I asked them to read their prior reflections and write a "Dear Reader" letter to introduce their portfolios to other teachers who would be reading them. Jennifer and Daniel wrote the following:

JENNIFER

Dear Reader,

Look on the writer side (of the portfolio) and you will see two copies of books. The two books are called Jennifer's Family. *My group watches me when I read [these books] to them.*

I have read over 30 books. I published 6 books. I published these two books a long time ago.

DANIEL

Dear Reader,

I want you to read Secrets of the Ninja. *It will be the first book you will see in my portfolio. Look on page 20 for dialect that I didn't know how to do at the beginning of 1st grade.*

I read over 30 books. I've published 8 books. 3 fact books. 5 fiction books. Five plus three is 8.

One additional component of the reflection process I will briefly mention. As part of an ongoing program of parent writing workshops, I invited parents to come to an evening meeting in which part of the agenda would include selecting and writing about a favorite piece from their child's writing folder. Mary Beth's mother brought a piece her child had written at home and added it to the portfolio. I encouraged parents to turn slowly through the pages of their child's work and to comment in every possible way. Most wrote a full-page letter to their children, glowing over content (I'm glad you included your brother), and style (I like the way you made the monster talk).

Will I continue my portfolio project? Yes, definitely. Portfolios represent the ultimate learning process: to know, to know that you know, and to know how you know. Will I conduct it in the same manner? Yes and no. I'll keep the open-ended reflection prompt because I have enjoyed trying to track down the concepts Mary Beth may have picked up from Bonn and those Bonn may have picked up from Kelly, and I have enjoyed seeing the concrete evidence of criteria for good writing my students have internalized. I want to study more carefully the idea that selection criteria might be linked to newly learned competencies as I believe the handwriting was. (What is the relationship between recently learning to write dialogue or metaphor and selecting a piece because it contains dialogue or metaphor?) I'll keep the parental involvement, but I'd like to expand it to include more parents and more selections. I also want to add a procedure in which students will respond to each other's portfolio because I believe it will magnify possibilities for them to learn from each other.

I dream that someone will ask me how I know my students are learning. I have my response prepared: because *they* know. They talk about learning with each other. They talk with me about their learning, and they reflect on learning when they write about the pieces they choose for their portfolios. Portfolios that are developed over time to include student-selected best works and insights about why each piece is valued by the writer yield a multilayered, three-dimensional view of mental growth. Reflection balances students on Vygotsky's (1978) edge of proximal development, the fine line between what students understand and what they are ready to learn, because it forces the deepest thinking of which they are capable at any given time. Portfolios let us see the best work of the student and his or her personal analysis of competence. Then, adding our own professional eye, we create a clearer picture of each student's growth and learning.

References

Cleary, B. 1960. *Ramona the Brave.* New York: Scholastic.

Dewey, J. 1916. *Democracy and Education.* New York: Macmillan.

Keats, E. J. 1973. *Skates.* New York: Franklin Watts.

Murphy, S., and M. A. Smith. 1991. *Writing Portfolios.* Markham, Ontario: Pippin.

Vygotsky, L. S. 1978. *Mind in Society.* Cambridge, MA: Harvard University Press.

The Small-*P* Portfolio Classroom

Patricia McGonegal

A Vermont teacher-leader for her state's portfolio program describes her alternate "homespun portfolio system" and the teaching strategies she uses to support it.

The current wave of reform movements seemed to wash over Vermont early, transmitting reform theory and practice in a way reminiscent of the game of telephone: the first teachers to hear about portfolio assessment had the clearest notion of the concept. Revised with each new telling, portfolio assessment and other valuable notions, however, can often go awry. They become unquestioned orthodoxy, they grow distorted, or they disappear.

Vermont's system of portfolio assessment began in 1989. Initially, those of us involved in this fledgling effort saw a portfolio as a collection of exemplary products developed by a student as he or she worked through a writing process. The state now demands six forms of writing from sixth- and eighth-graders: response to literature, report, personal essay, persuasive essay, narrative, and procedure. Many students produce remarkable collections, and many teachers accurately and clearly discern the level of achievement this writing reaches. But by spotlighting the forms, a "teach to the test" atmosphere seems to have developed, one that often short-circuits pieces in their development because a teacher must decide it is time to move on to practice the next required form.

While I am theoretically concerned about this tendency, I am a teacher of ninth- and tenth-graders and so far have been looking on the official portfolio process from a distance. Portfolio tools are available to me, but the assessment itself has not been imposed beyond grade eight.

The school where I teach, Mount Mansfield Union High School (MMU), is a cross section and a crossroads of Vermont. Twenty miles from Burlington, MMU has as diverse a student body as one can find in this whitest of states. Many families are employed by IBM, the University of Vermont, and local businesses. Some are farmers.

When I began at MMU in 1996, the apparent focus of the English curriculum was not writing but literature study. The majority of assigned writing in most classes could loosely be termed "literature response," with the obligatory research paper. Mindful of James Moffett's ironic claim that "the teaching of writing in America serves mostly to test reading [which] quite effectively kills two birds with one stone"(73), I have worked other forms of writing—narrative, poetry, and reflection, for instance—into our syllabus. I'm always negotiating between the school's canon, my own professional reading and experience, and large-scale administrative mandates. This negotiation has led to the development of what I call "portfolios with a small *p*."

I give out manila folders in September, saying, "Keep all your writing in this folder. Later on, you'll select the best pieces, and you'll be amazed at what you have there." I seldom use the term *portfolio,* as it carries negative connotations for some students, who cringe and moan when I mention the word. I assume that many of them come from classrooms where their teachers, mindful of the stakes and pressured by the "system," imposed the bottom-line genres on them. Writing in these classrooms was likely built around a brief tour through the six forms with an eye focused on the portfolio requirement. I also have some students who seem not to have heard the word *portfolio.* But I have others who have loved their writing and their portfolios. This may be because they love writing, loved the grade they've received on their portfolio assessment, or some of both. In any event, we can capitalize on the positive energy these students bring to our emerging writing community. Writing? Yes we like writing. Let's build on that.

In fact, in the small-*p* portfolio culture, we do not have to conduct a hasty tour through prescribed country. Not that we are leisurely, but we can take the time necessary to work through writing exercises, to study models, and to set our own standards for good writing and try them out. The upshot is that students actually have pieces worth selecting for a portfolio, pieces that show how much they have learned. It is this journey I want to describe here and, in particular, the kinds of teaching that can support portfolio assessment when the conditions allow.

A Small-*P* Portfolio Classroom

I do not begin the semester by diving right into the teaching of genres. Rather, I ask students to write for ten to fifteen minutes in response to a word I give them (it could be *numbers* or *change* or *school*). I have them read their pieces aloud to each other, then file these papers in folders. Without the pressure of a grade or even a rubric, students usually relax and even enjoy this writing and these read-aloud sessions. In the process, each student accumulates a varied batch of writing.

To understand why I've organized the first weeks of my class in this way, consider Steve. Steve is one of my ninth grade "basic" students, a "reluctant writer," but over a year's time, he will have accumulated as many as thirty short, lively writings—pieces that he found interesting, fruitful, and not a chore. Here is Steve writing in response to the word *numbers*:

> Numbers can be good in some ways. If we didn't have numbers, we wouldn't be able to use the phone the way we do now. Imagine a phone with letters not numbers. Also we wouldn't be able to see how fast we were going on the road and there would probably be more accidents. Also for timing some things (like cooking). Without numbers, there would either be serious problems or there would be something in its place. I also hate numbers. In math numbers screw me up in word

problems. Also I think it is dumb how they represent numbers on shows like Sesame Street. But the good side of it is that kids get a jump-start on learning about numbers.

A piece like this does not fit any of the genres that have been prescribed in the earlier grades by the state or any that is likely to be prescribed for high school portfolio assessment. If the genre had a name, James Britton's term *expressive writing* might be appropriate. Expressive writing is playful, exploratory writing that provides a level of comfort and success for both students and adults. In encouraging expressive writing, I also use short phrases ("What if" and "I notice" and "Is it just me?"), topics like "Suspension of the Students Caught Drinking" and "High School Schedules."

Do I want more from Steve than this piece of writing? Yes. I look toward his accumulated collection, a portfolio that will take these ideas and opinions and develop, revise, and maybe publish them.

An otherwise quiet student, Jacob shows how much he is thinking about when he writes expressively:

Is it just me, or do parents like having you do homework on the weekends? Monday, Tuesday, Wednesday, Thursday, and Friday we do a tremendous amount of homework. I believe we should have weekends off like working adults do. We have a 6.5-hour day of school and adults have an 8-hour day. We also have between an hour to 2.5 hours of homework a night. That makes our day 7.5 to 9 hours a day. That's more than the average adult. On top of that we have a good two hours of homework every weekend. Their average week is 40 hours, but our week is 43.3 hours on average. If weekend homework were cut, we would almost be even.

This writing might seem skimpy to a portfolio reader evaluating it as a persuasive essay, but as a beginning, as a starting place to be developed, it is an exploration rich in potential. I believe that students like Jacob will grow faster and go further as writers beginning with a prompt like "Is it just me" than with a rubric of points to be evaluated on a persuasive essay.

Beyond Freewriting

As the semester moves on, I try to direct writing assignments to support our grade level expectations for our students. Small-*p* portfolio classrooms can accommodate a range of writing experiences, including those that an English department has deemed important. For instance, our ninth grade students are expected to begin work with research papers, a genre that in my classroom begins with more freewriting.

One year, for example, we explored students' visions for their future as a research focus. They read and wrote to explore a profession or a location of which they had dreamed. This journey began with freewriting in which students envisioned a future job or location. Here are Trevor's first thoughts:

> It's dark and hot, and the crowd sounds like an ocean. They say there are over 10,000 people here tonight, and that this is the biggest concert ever documented. 4, 3, 2, 1 the music starts and I can feel the adrenaline pumping through my veins. Faster and faster we play. I feel like the music will never stop. Four hours later, it's over, the ocean now depleting to a river. My friends and I are totally satisfied by how this event has gone. This is where I want to be!
>
> Since the beginning of time, there has been music. There have been good bands and bad bands. I want to be up at the top with those good bands. But I would like to know, what is the best route for me to go if I want to become a better musician? I'd like to know what are the best music schools, the best musician to get advice from and what kind of drumset would benefit me most.

For Trevor, this freewrite begins as a wish-filled daydream but ends with some specific questions that will send his research in a fruitful direction. From these beginnings, students go on to fulfill the research expectations of the English department. Most of them do some real digging into sources, finding out things they feel a real need to know. I believe that because of the exploratory writing that jump-started these projects, much of their language will stay alive, honest, and interesting to read.

As the year passes, we explore other forms of writing. I often choose freewriting prompts with an eye on form and subject matter. For instance, at the time we were reading *Julius Caesar* we were also working on the persuasive essay form. Every couple of weeks my students look at their freewritings and choose one piece to develop. During this time, I prompted students to respond to words such as *honor, heroes, friendship,* and *superstition,* all topics that can be augmented by the plot and text of *Julius Caesar.* We write narratives when we read short stories; personal essays when we read *Ordinary People, Diary of Anne Frank,* and *The Miracle Worker;* poetry when we read poetry.

Models

All of this takes time. In the current atmosphere of "hurry up and learn," I believe too much attention gets paid to directions and strategies for executing a form and not enough attention to providing students with examples of what they are trying to achieve. I show models of both student-authored and professional pieces. Anna Quindlen and Donald Murray's writings teach my students a lot about informal essays, and sometimes I see them borrowing these authors' techniques and styles, just as I do. Editorials and op-ed pieces can model the persuasive essay. I save student work from year to year, and these writings inspire some students more than any other type of model or instruction.

Models show my students the value of length. In early "writing workshop" days, I was afraid to impose length expectations on my students, and I sincerely promised them that I valued the quality, not the amount of writing. What did this get me? Many short pieces. Still hesitant to dictate length in most papers, I take an end run. I let students see the value of Anna Quindlen's stories within her essays. I am soon getting back small vignettes that fill out the pieces. Here is an illustration of a vignette included in this argument for improved lockers:

> *Annie rushed up before English class to retrieve her lit book. In her haste, she left the door open and hurried off. Sammy, straigtening up from his "lower" locker, connected with the sharp door of Annie's, splitting open a gash on his cheek.*

I wonder if Carla could so deftly have caught the character of the boss in her Vietnam story if she had not experienced the details that Judith Guest uses to delineate character in *Ordinary People*. Carla writes:

> I went numb quite fast, and I could barely talk an hour after the telegram told us the bad news. "Take the rest of the day off, Ginger," said my boss. "You'll need some time to help with your cousin's funeral."

In short, students like Carla and Annie, if they are not so overburdened with genre writing, can take the time they need for the reading that can make them better writers.

Judging and Responding

So far, the portfolio rubrics used in Vermont have been handed to us by the state. For the small-*p* portfolio, I want students to try to develop rubrics, and models can be a big help in this process. Looking at the student or professional pieces, I ask students with each new form, "What makes a good one of these?" And because they have immersed themselves in models of this form, they know. For narrative writing, students identify, for example, clear, precise language, a "grabby" lead, details that keep the reader reading, characters who change. I write these on the board and show students Vermont's rubric for this form of writing, and we find similarities. The narrative rubric, for example, calls for writing that

- presents main character effectively
- maintains a clear topic and focus
- creates a believable world dramatizing rather than telling what happens
- shows character growth and change.

Even though the two rubrics substantially overlap, a list of qualities that comes first from the students and then is confirmed by the higher powers seems to me and the students a more authentic way to proceed than simply accepting a rubric from afar.

Models and rubrics help students develop a language for responding to one another's work, and they inspire students to revise their own work. When I ask students to respond to one another's pieces, I borrow a device from my son's teacher Bob Brown. In the span of a period, students spend fifteen minutes typing their work into a computer. With fifteen minutes left, they save their work and move to a different computer terminal. They read, change the font on their neighbor's terminal, and write a response. If there's time, we go a second round, with the second reader responding both to the piece and the first response. This process increases engagement, strengthens the sense of a writing community, and gives writers valuable peer feedback. Students save the feedback, and this helps me see and design mini-lessons on skill, revision, and conference techniques.

Writing folders store all these pieces, with feedback from students and from me, until May, when we select the best work, and the folder becomes a portfolio.

Responding, Then Assessing

These student-developed rubrics also play a major role in assessing what students have accomplished. Students first assess a finished piece using a genre-specific rubric provided by the state. This rubric describes elements of good essays or narratives, reinforcing and enriching the standards we have determined together. I then add my own feedback, pointing out the strong and weak points I see in their papers. I don't give a number or a letter grade for the writing, only credit for completion.

Assembling a Portfolio

Over the year, we have looked at various genres, freewriting our way through them, moving our freewriting toward developed pieces that may be "keepers" at year's end, and building this community of writers who question, affirm, resist, and/or respond to one another. Now, as we round the bend into the final stretch, we begin consciously to use "the *p* word." It's time to take stock. I ask students to put together a portfolio. After all the freewritings and revisions and all the close readings and rubrics and responses, what is important enough to keep? I don't pretend that it will count as part of their college transcript, since as of now it won't. I don't tell them that it will go on to be read carefully by next year's teachers, as would be the case in another educational universe, because this is simply not going to happen.

With a month of school left, I ask students to sort through their writing folders and pick a collection that showcases their best work. "Show us who you are as a writer: a storyteller, an explorer of your thoughts and others', a person with opinions and convictions." I ask them to choose one finished work from each of four forms—informal essay, persuasive essay, narrative, and research writing—and arrange them in a clean new folder for my review and for their parents to review as well.

Reflection

Unfortunately, though reflection was a key ingredient in the portfolio as the original reformers conceived the idea, this personal analysis is not now part of our state-mandated assessment. On the other hand, the small-*p* portfolio expects reflection from these young writers. As students select pieces to include in their collection, we take one class session to attach a simple "Entry Form" to each piece. The two prompts on this form are meant to inspire reflection. One is headed, "This piece is included in my portfolio because . . . " and the other, "A reader should notice . . .".

I send this note home to parents, asking them to look over and comment on the work of their child:

Dear Parents,

Enclosed is the selected work collection (portfolio) of your son or daughter's writing from this school year. . . . Please take some time this weekend and look through your child's work, and share your observations with us on the enclosed parent feedback form. Feel free to use any of the criteria we have used or write your own observations of what you see here (strengths, "challenges," growth, or any other qualities of this writing).

Some parents respond to this request, and their level of analysis is heartening. Some of the students have two parents looking together at their work and joining in the conversation:

Liz's strength, I think, lies in creative writing. Her poems and stories seem to flow and have more "energy" than her other writings. She still seems to need to work on proofreading.   —Liz's mother

Liz's original writings seem to operate on a more mature level than her reports and reactions/reflections. Her use of vocabulary and metaphor, e.g. are much more developed. Perhaps she should learn to write more "creatively" even in her nonfiction and reports.

—Liz's father

Carla wrote diligently and cheerfully all year. Her accomplishments are applauded by her mother, who has been supporting her all along:

Carla's writing is beginning to flourish and shows her feelings about things that are important to her. She makes you feel as though you are right there with her doing whatever she is doing. —Carla's mother

Carla wrote a cover letter that confirmed her mother's judgment.

I believe that my portfolio this year reveals who I am as a writer and as a person. My portfolio shows how I have progressed over the school year and how my literacy skills have grown. I feel that my work truly has purpose. Even when I was told to write a procedure piece, I made it something that I cared about and truly wanted to write.

In all of my pieces, I have tried to apply the skills which I have learned in class and enhance my writing and make it more interesting to read. I have added in descriptions, detail, and figurative language in many places. I believe that my voice and stance is appropriately shown throughout my writing. By reading my work, one can understand how I feel about a given topic. I have been organized through all my writing steps to a completed work. My pieces of

writing are placed thoughtfully in my portfolio. . . . Along with many
writing assignments, I worked on independent pieces such as poetry
and personal narratives throughout the school year. This summer I
plan to continue writing.

This year, I have found inside myself my love for literature, poetry
and writing. . . . The world around me influences my writing in many
ways. This summer, I think that if I continue writing, I will come back
in the Fall with many productive pieces and will have secured my
newly found inspiration. I would like to continue writing when I leave
high school, and plan to minor, if not take a career in literature in
the future.

A Portfolio at Last

The students and I assemble our own collection each year, a small-*p*
portfolio, which we can shape to our own needs and interests, in some
respects, yet still compare to and assess against the directives from the
Department of Education. I wouldn't impose our system on others,
although I'd recommend that elements of it might be tried by some
other teachers and their students.

The small-*p* portfolio is complex and unpredictable, messy and
chaotic. I have described the process here in some detail to contrast the
work-in-progress document that a portfolio should be with the numbers game assessment that portfolios are in danger of becoming.

When the dust settles and the last-day-party stickiness has been
washed off the desks, I'm left with lots of issues to dive back into for
next year. As I continue to treasure my homespun portfolio system,
what role should I play in the formation of a high school portfolio
assessment? Can it be fashioned in a way that increases attention to
many forms of writing in the high school, as it has, at its best, in the elementary and middle levels? Or will it become a stress-filled administrative tool, owned by the system, not the student?

My students don't all achieve splendor. They leave me as diverse as
when they came, some ready next year to experiment and grow with
writing, some to await instruction and perform for a grade, others to

bear each class period and sidestep involvement as much as possible. But their definition of *portfolio* has been revised, and their visions of themselves have been explored, developed, and honored.

References

Moffett, James. 1988. *Coming on Center: Essays in English Education.* Portsmouth, NH: Heinemann.

Portfolios That Make a Difference: A Four-Year Journey

Judith Ruhana

An Illinois middle-school teacher recounts her history with classroom portfolios. She remains impressed and humbled by her students' insights into their own writing.

What do you know about portfolios?" This question came from the human services director interviewing me for the job I now have. "Absolutely nothing!" I thought.

But I wanted the job so I made something up—quickly. I knew that in art, a portfolio is a collection gathered together to show off the artist's best work, so I transferred this definition to language arts: "It's a collection of writing gathered together to show the student's ability," I said.

My stab at an explanation must have been good enough because I got the job; however, that question "What do you know about portfolios?" did not go away. Rather, it started me on a year-long quest to find out as much as I could. I read everything I could get my hands on.

In the end, I decided that portfolios had nothing to do with me. I convinced myself that all those classrooms using portfolios were not full of normal kids, were not public schools, did not have heterogeneous groupings, did not have minorities, did not have English language learners or bilingual students, did not have 33 percent of the population on free and reduced lunches, did not have normal teachers. Teaching in the "real world" made the very thought of portfolios seem overwhelming. I had no idea how to get started.

I teach in Nichols Middle School in Evanston, Illinois, a public, urban, multicultural school with many disadvantaged students. I have six classes of language arts—writing only—and about 125 students. How could I deal with portfolio assessment? The sheer volume of papers required to carry out this process with all these students seemed daunting. I wouldn't even be able to store all that paper.

But events overtook my objections. I wanted to put out an end-of-the-year student literary magazine, and for this project I needed to collect and store student work. I managed the logistics of this undertaking with enough ease that I began again to consider portfolios for my classroom.

Year One

During the summer, I figured out a system. Every student would have a large plastic folder for the storage of his or her work, and each class would place these folders in six different colored milk crates—one crate per period. With this class management problem solved, I could now think about the "what," "how," and "why" of portfolio assessment. I soon realized that my problem had never been with the "why." From the time I started my investigation, I was convinced that portfolios were a form of good practice that led to authentic assessment. My concerns had been the "how." I needed a model.

The model I chose came from the Kentucky Department of Education (appendix A). Kentucky requires that eighth-graders select five pieces of work from their year's worth of writing. Although any of the entries may come from study areas other than English/language arts, a minimum of one piece must come from another study area. The portfolio requirement includes: one personal narrative, one piece of fiction, and one personal selection. In addition, two pieces of the portfolio should contain writing that achieves one or more of the following purposes: predicts an outcome; defends a position; analyzes a situation, person, place, or thing; solves a problem; explains a process or concept; draws a conclusion; or creates a model.

Each student is also required to write a letter reflecting on his or her growth as a writer and on the pieces in the portfolio. Good. A letter I could handle. Compared to the formal research paper students write in the spring as part of a huge interdisciplinary unit, a letter would be easier to evaluate and more interesting for me to read.

I had the program in place in September. I showed the students the portfolio requirements the first month of school and encouraged but did not demand that they save all their work—both good and not so good—in their classroom portfolios.

At the end of the year, students enjoyed writing the reflective letter to me, their last say on what they did that year in my class. I liked the letter format because students already had experience with letter writing, and even the students who found writing difficult felt secure in writing a letter to their teacher.

What I didn't realize or expect was the ease with which my students looked at their own work, what they already knew about their writing, and how their perspectives helped my understanding of them. Portfolio assessment opened channels of communication with them that were both real and profound. This experiment gave students their own voice in my classroom, and I found myself listening.

Students were helping me better understand the connection between their topic and the quality of their writing.

Writing about something that was very personal and emotional to me made my writing more effective. When your heart is really part of something, I think you can write about it better because you really understand and feel the emotions you are trying to express. —Iyesha

I chose this narrative essay . . . because I really hated it and I didn't get a good grade on it. This essay was really hard for me to write about because I don't like the topic and it wasn't really true because I made up a lot of it. Another reason why I didn't like writing this was because I don't like writing things that really happened. If I have to tell about

*things that really happened I never tell them so that they sound as
good as they were. I feel like what's the point if it doesn't sound as
good as it really was?*   —Martha

Some wrote confessions that they might have had trouble making
face-to-face:

*I am sorry to say that I rushed this assignment, putting no effort into
it whatsoever.... I had no intention of doing a good job. There was not
enough information and it was very brief for a report.... I chose this
writing so that it could remind me to devote more time and effort to
my assignments.*   —Jose

*Another weakness of this paper was I didn't have very much time to
write it because I had to go to Florida the next day. This is the reason I
had to turn it in early and didn't have time to think about it.* —Martha

But other students complained, and, as is true for many teachers, the
complaints were what grabbed my attention.

*How can you expect me to remember what I did writing this piece
when all I can remember is that I got an F!*   —Ben

*I couldn't find anything in my portfolio that was from another subject
and the teachers were mad at me when I asked them for old work!*
                                                          —Julia

*I don't have enough work to choose from so why are you making us
do this? —Anne*

I don't know how to reflect on my own work. Isn't that your job?
                                                          —Chad

Ben was right. What was the point of asking students to reflect on
some piece they had composed several months ago and hardly remem-
bered writing?

Julia and Anne were right. My directions had been vague. I "encourage" students to save their work, but this kind of mild suggestion often
washes right by middle school students, who have plenty of other things
on their minds.

And, finally, Chad was right. I had never taught students how to reflect, and even if I did not agree with Chad that reflecting on student work was entirely my responsibility and not theirs, if I expected students to think about their writing and themselves as writers, I needed to teach them how and why to do this work.

I realized that these student reflections went beyond insights into their writing; they were also comments on my teaching practices. To the extent that these practices reflected my poor planning, I vowed to change.

Year Two

Having Enough Work to Choose from:
Learning from Julia and Anne

Before the next school year began, I persuaded the other team teachers for our grade level to cooperate in gathering writing pieces for my students. Sometimes these teachers gave me written pieces, sometimes I copied the pieces and they kept them, and sometimes they gave the work to the students to put in their language-arts portfolios. We core teachers —literature, language arts, social studies, science—began to communicate more on writing across the curriculum, and the students began to apply what they learned in language arts to their other subjects. The students would often moan, "Oh, no, you're looking at our writing in the other subjects, too," and "That's terrible!" What they meant was, "Oh, no, we have to write effectively in all the subjects now!"

Another simple change I made at the onset of the second year was to tell students that they could never take their portfolios out of the classroom, not even to their lockers. The portfolio envelopes remained in my classroom all year; students could borrow work to take home and show off to parents, but they had to return it. Team members also kept work that students might need for their portfolios. The watchwords for both students and teachers became "Never Throw Anything Away."

Knowing How to Reflect on Your Work: Learning from Chad

Early in September of the second year, I refined the reflection process. The students and I spent one entire class brainstorming a list of questions that students could use to look at their own work reflectively. The students kept the list in their portfolios throughout the year:

- How did you grow as a writer?

- What was hard? Easy?

- What did you enjoy the most? The least?

- Why and how did you make the changes you made in this piece?

- Looking at this piece now, what would you change?

- What piece would you do over and why?

Remembering the Process for Each Document: Learning from Ben

Every six or eight weeks, we had two or three "portfolio days" devoted to finding writing pieces and doing mini-assessments on them. On these portfolio days, students took index cards, jotted responses to some of the reflection questions, and stapled the cards to their work.

By the end of the year, in May, when I assigned students the formal evaluation letter, they were really ready to look at their work. Their portfolio collection included work in all subjects. Their notations on index cards helped them remember the process and problems involved with each piece. They had pieces they loved and pieces they hated. They could learn from both their successes and their failures. Particularly, students seemed aware of the forms and subject matter that led to their best writing.

So far, poetry has been the best outlet for my real emotions. Poetry has helped me grow as a writer very much. . . . I do my best writing when I have strong feelings—especially negative feelings—about my subject. Most other kinds of writing are about a topic or assignment that is given to you. Teachers can't really tell you what to write about in a poem. Poetry comes from the heart; no research is needed.—Graham

I do best in big projects, like the Civil War Project, because I am good at organizing things over a long period of time. It's the essays that I stink at because I can't get organized that fast. Maybe I need to give myself more time to outline or something. —Ellen

However, one reflection question students consistently avoided: "How have you grown as a writer?" Those who tried to answer had little notion of how to respond. There were a great many "My grades got better" (or worse) and "I did more things this year." A couple of sentences in Brandon's reflection gave a clue as to why this was happening:

I can never figure out the categories we have to choose for this letter. I didn't really know how to write it. —Brandon

So even though we had developed the prompts to help students reflect, the concept of "growing" as a writer was still difficult for them to grasp.

Year Three

How to Write the Letter: Learning from Brandon

I reasoned that if students were to analyze their growth as writers they would need to keep the evidence of this growth as it was occurring. I began by insisting that students save all drafts and prewriting to turn in with final copies. Their ever-growing portfolios now contained work in all stages of progress to help them trace their change and growth. I also asked students to write a letter at the beginning of the year as well as at the end—another demonstration of growth.

This early letter had four requirements: a short autobiography of their writing habits and projects, a paragraph on their strengths and weaknesses as writers, their goals in writing for the year, and their comments on the curriculum, a copy of which had been posted on the wall. These letters were written in tones that reflected anticipation as well as some dread:

I can't wait to get to the science fiction unit. I heard about how great it was from last year's class, and I have already started my story.
—Erika

I have no idea what a writing workshop is but I hope it's not poetry. I can never seem to relate to poems let alone write them!　—Laura

Now in the third year of my portfolio immersion, I began to realize that some of the problems students were having with reflection came from the fact that I was allowing them to skim the surface. For instance, some would state their reasons for choosing a particular piece and let it go at that, without analyzing those reasons. So during one class, just before students began writing their letters, I modeled the process for them by writing reflective comments on my own work. Choosing three questions from our list, I wrote my thoughts on an overhead projector so students could comment on the results as they saw them unfold. The students were all too happy to evaluate my writing. My first draft reflection read:

I chose this piece because I was struck by three things. First, and most importantly, I chose nonfiction. Second, writing is for me an exercise in memory; and lastly, I really love my piece.　—Me

The students enjoyed telling me that this paragraph was really ineffective. They had me rewrite it several times so that it began to look much different:

As I gathered work for this portfolio I looked at this poem that was a big hit with the students. I realized how much I loved writing nonfiction because it was an exercise in memory. I found myself remembering my father all over again as I wrote about our Saturday nights together. "Daddy's Saturday Nights" is my first portfolio choice because it made me cry. I revised it four times and it changed dramatically as it went through these revisions.　—Me

However, both the students and I remained dissatisfied with this still-sketchy analysis. As students continued to probe the reason I liked this piece so much, I found I could best respond by quoting the work.

"He came in with the apron in a bag—ready for the wash— and with fatigue pulling at the corners of his mouth and eyes, making his steps drag and his body loose with the kind of tiredness that numbs." This

image of my dad just seemed to flow out of my pen while I was writing this piece and I felt like he was here again. Maybe that's why I love nonfiction writing so much.   —Me

Once I modeled the technique of referring to the text, students had no trouble using this device in their own letters.

I loved my short story written for Writers' Workshop. "People always left David alone because he pushed them away. He did this because he was plagued by his own gift. David saw right through himself not liking what he saw. David masked himself under many layers of false identities. Not knowing where the real him was anymore, David stopped trying to find himself." That was one of my favorite parts. I chose this because it shows what some people are really like: they don't (know) what is the real them.   —Alissa

The descriptive elements, such as similes and metaphors in this observational essay make the event come alive. However, my favorite line of this essay is when I said, "She had black hair French braided down the middle of her head and was waiting impatiently for the show to start like a small kindergartener waiting for her milk." This piece of writing intrigues me every time I read it, which makes this one of my best pieces.   —Bess

During this third year in May, I gave students the assessment rubric (appendix B) before they started their letters. They evaluated their work using the rubric, and then I evaluated the work on the same sheet of paper they used: side-by-side evaluations. I found that if they evaluated their work first, they found things they had overlooked and changed them before they turned in the final copy. I also set aside time for them to use the rubric in class two days prior to the letter due date so that it would be done thoughtfully. They often worked in teams to revise their work, and some comments from these peer reviews made students revise their letters so that their work was more thoughtful and exceeded the standard. Some sample peer comments:

"This paragraph doesn't answer questions—for example, 'How did you grow?'"

"Tell what the writing is, and explain by using the text."

"Put in what you accomplished this year and what you didn't as your second-to-last paragraph."

This year, in contrast to former years, students had more tools to help them reflect on their work. They took out their September letters as examples of their own process of growth and change and as the rubric by which they would be assessed. Then they worked in groups to edit their letters prior to handing them in.

Students were reflecting on their work and discovering new things about it and themselves in a way they had not been doing in earlier years. Some of their reflections and the works they refer to are amazingly insightful, even poetic:

> *Another piece that I really enjoyed writing and probably out of all the works I have created was the one that meant the most to me was "Sunset." I remembered taking walks on the beach in the late afternoon when the sun was just getting ready to sink beneath the waves. I remembered watching as the colors mixed and changed into a heavenly daze as the sun dug into the horizon. I remembered watching for the green flash of light that would fan out across the horizon in a final moment of glory as if to say farewell before it dove into the quiet waters of the Gulf.*
>
> > *Sunset is beautiful. Rich and enchanting. Parading across the sky. The colors ripple across with deep motion, digging into the bottom of your soul and finding your old favorite memories.*
> > *Then as the(y) slide into the ocean, dripping wet they drown into a pool of blue. The finale is about to begin as the last delicate stroke of fine color slips into the sea.* —Paul

> *I know for a fact that this will be a powerful letter because I usually keep personal things to myself and the first letter I wrote was not that personal and this time I am going to get personal. The pieces I have chosen are works that help people know how I see the world and how I see myself.* —Martin

Students reported growth not only in the way they were coming to know about and use rhetorical tools but also in their willingness to open up to topics, forms, and audiences they would not always have been willing or able to approach:

The piece that speaks my true voice is the poem "Hate" because it was a combination of what I had seen in real life, on television, and what I was thinking about.... Sometimes I even start to cry for no reason at all because I am thinking about something related to hate. I like that I finally wrote how I feel about this topic and that I can share my feelings without being criticized.... This piece defines my contribution to the genre by showing that you can write anything in poetry. —Dean

I don't think I have to introduce myself, I did that in September. I'm the one who can never meet a deadline, I can't spell, and I always had trouble getting things formatted from my computer to the ones at school. Death to Macs! Somehow I actually met my goals for the year. I got at least two things in the Lit Mag, I won a contest, and I found my true voice! —Susan

And many students were able to step back and take the long view of where they once were as writers and where they are now.

Frankly I think that over the past two years, I have become a writer. The fall of seventh grade I came in having no idea how to write a good essay, short story or term paper. I felt that I was required to write what I thought you would like. As I wrote more and more, I learned to be creative, to write from my heart and take my chance. —Chris

I used to get scared when you gave us writers workshop. I never had any ideas at the beginning of the year. I even thought poetry was my favorite kind of writing because it seemed so easy. Now, I've grown as a writer and realize that I am a short story kind of gal, especially sci-fi. —Amy

Reflecting on my own growth as a teacher, at the end of three years, I could hold up pieces such as these as evidence that my students were now much more enthusiastic participants in the portfolio process.

However, as anyone who has taught may have anticipated, there were still rumbles of discontent—mostly about grades:

> *At the start of every school year, I try my hardest to do an excellent job on every paper to give teachers the idea that I have excellent work habits. But for some reason this year I am getting the lowest grades I have ever received in my whole school career. I hate portfolio days because I have to look at all those bad grades. Can you help me about this? Thanks for letting me blab in this paragraph.* —John

> *Why didn't you tell me I was doing this bad? I would have changed.* —Max

> *I really think I am a really good poet when I am not pressured into things like due dates and that kind of stuff. So all I am saying is that I would have gotten a better grade if I had a little more time to think about things.* —Christa

Once again these critical comments inspired change for the coming year.

Year Four

What could I do about these concerns? I decided I needed a more fluid approach to grading. Students needed to be able to revise their writing to raise their grades.

The biggest change was that after "portfolio days," which occurred every six to eight weeks and were devoted to finding and assessing writing pieces, students had a week for revision. Many students did not like their work or their grades and were not aware of how badly they were doing until we set aside those few days to review all their writing. They could change their grades or evaluations by redoing, rethinking, revising, or just editing their work. When I gave them this time, I found that they were happier about writing and felt more in control of their own grades and their own growth.

Every year as I make my plans, I make sure to specify times and dates for portfolio assessment and for portfolio rewrite days. I make sure that

I have days and times when students can discuss their reflections with me before I evaluate the portfolios. Students experience their own voices, and I hear them in a whole new way. When I read their letters, I am often humbled and moved by what students discover about themselves and their writing.

> *I had this piece forming in my head all summer.... When we were assigned to write in any genre we wanted I set out, determined to write down my story and pull it off. About one hundred revisions later, I had a garbage full of crumpled paper, a notebook damaged from being hurled across the room in frustration, and my story. While writing this letter, I learned that if I pick a creative way to do an assignment or a good topic to do it on, I will enjoy the process of writing it and the final product will be better.* —Charles

> *Throughout the year, we have accomplished writing many different types of papers. But I believe that my best and most effective piece of writing was at the beginning of the year, which was about my grandmother living with me and later her stay at the hospital. The reason why this was effective was that it brought out feelings about that time that I had never expressed.... I learned that if you have experienced something, you can write about it and make it seem more real. For example, the descriptions of my grandmother were good because I could see her in my mind so clearly, and it was therefore easy to write an accurate description. Also, because I was writing about my grandmother, I made an extra effort to make this paper good. It was almost as if I was writing a memorial to her, and I wanted her to be proud of me.... Writing this piece made me feel like a real author.* —Daniel

In the three years since its inception, portfolio assessment in May has become my favorite time of the school year because during the two weeks this process takes, students talk to me on a level that amazes both me and them. They enjoy the process of choosing work for reflection, and they are able to see things in their work and their writing that I missed and they missed the first time around. Most wonderful, they see their own growth as writers, as students, as people, and they realize that education is a journey. They learn that reflection matters.

References

Kentucky Department of Education. *KIRIS Writing Portfolio Assessment: Contents of the Grade 8 Portfolio.* Frankfort, KY: Kentucky Department of Education.

Porter, Carol, and Janell Cleland. 1995. *The Portfolio as a Learning Strategy.* Portsmouth, NH: Heinemann-Boynton/Cook.

Appendix A

KIRIS Writing Portfolio Assessment

Contents of the Grade 8 Portfolio

Any of the following portfolio entries may come from study areas other than English/Language Arts, but a minimum of *one* piece of writing *must* come from another study area.

Table of Contents: Include the title or descriptor of each portfolio entry, the study area for which the piece was written, and the page number in the portfolio.

1. A Letter to the Reviewer: A letter written by the student discussing his/her growth as a writer and reflecting on the pieces in the portfolio.
2. One Personal Narrative
3–4. Two Pieces of Writing, each of which achieves any one or more of the following purposes:
    a. Predict an Outcome
    b. Defend a Position
    c. Analyze or Evaluate a Situation, Person, Place, or Thing
    d. Solve a Problem
    e. Explain a Process or Concept
    f. Draw a Conclusion
    g. Create a Model
5. One Short Story, Poem, Play/Script, or other piece of Fiction
6. A Personal Selection: One additional piece of writing that the student wishes to include.

Used with permission of the Kentucky Department of Education, Frankfort, Kentucky 40601

Appendix B

Rubric for Portfolio Assessment

_____10 Does the reader of the portfolio get a sense of how you have changed as a writer?

_____10 Does the reader understand why you chose each piece?

_____10 Does the portfolio explain what you have learned about yourself as a writer?

_____10 Has your portfolio been shared with someone else for a response?

_____10 Is the form correct?

_____10 Is the writing clear and error free?

_____10 Is the reflection honest and does your voice come through?

_____10 Neatness

_____10 Completeness

_____10 On time

_____100 Total

Reprinted from *The Portfolio as a Learning Strategy* by Porter and Cleland. Copyright © 1995. Published by Heinemann, a divison of Reed Elsevier Inc., Portsmouth, NH. All rights reserved.

The Birth and Death of Portfolio Assessment 1992–2000

Pauline Sahakian

A veteran teacher recalls "the good old days" of creating a school portfolio program, only to watch it crumble as conditions changed.

One by one the soon-to-graduate students at Buchanan High School in Clovis, California, file to the front of the room. As they read from what they consider the best work in their portfolios, they beam with pride. Today is Senior Showcase Portfolio Day.

Sadly, however, Senior Showcase Portfolio Day is all too aptly named. Through no fault of the student readers, this event has become a show, a kind of charade. Indeed, the use of portfolios in my school has withered to a state of show-and-tell with students collecting work each year to put in a folder accompanied by a superficial introduction essay. I say "superficial" because most essays lack any insight into how their portfolios demonstrate their writing processes or how their writing and thinking are improving. An excerpt from a typical tenth grade essay:

My writing really improved a lot this year and I worked hard to make it happen. I tried to correct all of my mistakes. I notice that I'm making fewer mistakes and my essays are longer. In my first essay I wrote

about my mother. My friend said it was really good. Maybe it was
good because I really love my mother. I hope you like this essay.

Of course, many students offer far greater insight into their work, but too many make no attempt to reflect on their growth or provide the reader with evidence to demonstrate progress. They give no examples, make no comparisons, and draw few conclusions. Not uncommonly, they depend on mechanical transitions of "my next essay," "my third," and so on, offering the reader no sense that the writer has actually thought about what she or he has learned. But to blame the other students for these perfunctory performances would be to blame the victims. These students cannot be held responsible for what they have not been taught. Neither would it be reasonable to blame the teachers. They also have not been taught. Almost none of them were around in 1992 when a group of us were won over to the then-revolutionary concept of portfolio assessment. We became committed to the idea that portfolio assessment could shed light on the invisible: the struggles, the small steps forward, the intellectual progress over time. We spent many hours wrestling with the means to achieve these lofty ends.

The teachers who came along later had had no part in this dialogue. For them, students just weren't getting it. "The kids just don't know how to reflect. So why are we doing this?" they would ask. "Isn't this really too much work for what we're getting out of it?" I do not believe they would be asking these questions if they had been with us in 1992. At the risk of romanticizing some golden age of literacy education now obscured in the mists of time, I want to recall our work in that year and the years following.

The Birth Process

A new high school had been built in my district in California's central valley, and I was returning to the classroom after seven years of being a teacher on special assignment. "A perfect opportunity," I had said to a close colleague and friend, Joan. We had often talked about what we would do if we were in charge of the educational world. Now was our chance. The principal, who also believed the time had come for change, hired us along with four others. Jake, Nan, Joan, and I were veteran National Writing Project teacher-consultants, Dave was working on his thesis for a master's degree, and Dawn, the youngest member, had taught in another district for five years.

Our work began in August—a long week of trying to come together. After setting our goals for the department and reviewing the curriculum, Joan and I suggested we design a portfolio system to help us meet our goal of improving student writing. In our enthusiasm we both started talking at the same time, wanting to tell our stories of what we had learned about portfolios, our voices stepping on each other's, perhaps mine being shamelessly the louder.

I had attended an inservice workshop for the San Joaquin Valley Writing Project (SJVWP), at which Mary Ann Smith (then co-director of the Bay Area Writing Project) demonstrated from her work at Mt. Diablo High School that much can be learned about teaching writing by looking at students' writing over time. I shared my excitement about Mary Ann's presentation, and in fact, all of the teachers on our team had either read about or heard about this new concept and were ready to give it a try.

To move our process forward, Joan suggested we write for fifteen minutes about why we would want to assess student writing through portfolios. When we shared our quick-writes, we gave surprisingly similar reasons. We believed that we could see what students were actually learning if we compared early work to later work. We believed we could determine which assignments were well presented and which were confusing. We believed students would be able to see their progress in fluency and idea development and be inspired to work harder, that they could focus their problem solving if they saw patterns of repetition in their writing. We concluded that the more students were required to think about how they wrote, the more their writing would improve. After much discussion, we ultimately settled on two purposes for our portfolio design: we wanted students to see how they were growing as writers and thinkers from their freshman to senior year, and we hoped to collect information on how well we were teaching our curriculum.

Although defining our purposes for using portfolios brought a peaceful close to our first day together, we did not see eye to eye about how to accomplish these purposes. For the next three days, our philosophical differences about design and process came to light. Dave wanted a tight structure for students with a prepared list of every assignment required for the end-of-the-year portfolio. "It needs to show administrators and parents what we are teaching," he insisted. Jake was more concerned about ownership. He argued that the portfolios belonged to the students, not to us, and therefore should consist of only their choices.

We debated the merits of these opposing views for an entire morning. Joan, whom we later called "O Thoughtful One," came back from lunch with an idea. She explained that if we truly wanted to give students ownership and choices, while we gleaned information about our assignments, they needed to write several pieces in different genres. In this way, we would identify categories from which they could choose while ensuring that the work revealed the types of writing we were teaching (journal writing, response writing, narrative writing, interpretive writing, argument, and so on).

"Won't that take a lot of time?" Dawn asked, which launched us into ways to weave writing into the study of literature. From these conversations, we began to realize how a portfolio system was going to change not only how we assessed students but also how we taught. The hard work lay ahead in our daily and weekly planning.

To achieve our first purpose, that students see and think about their growth, we agreed to include all drafts of process papers and to provide opportunities for students to select what they thought was their best work each quarter. Dave suggested they write a "letter to the reader," while the rest of us preferred a reflective essay format. His argument for letter format was based on his belief that a letter might be less intimidating. The rest of us argued that an informal letter would not encourage the kind of reflection we intended to teach. After another hour of debate, we settled on the letter format for ninth-graders and the reflective essay writing for tenth-graders. At the same time, we reminded one another that whatever we decided was certainly not carved in stone.

But we were wrong. For all practical purposes, our work was carved in stone. Other than creating a rubric that fall for scoring the end-of-the-year portfolios and eliminating, at the end of two years, the bulkiness that came with too many drafts, we never again questioned the process or design. We felt some guilt about this, but we thought we had an excuse. Our new school was growing so fast, with so many new teachers, that finding a time when everyone could meet became difficult. So we simply gave up. Our innovative school settled into being not so innovative.

The Inevitable Death

Eight years later, only two of our original six teachers are still teaching in the department, and twenty or more new teachers have since been hired. As a department, we no longer discuss student learning. Instead, we talk about raising test scores. The spirit of inquiry that characterized our little band of explorers metamorphosed into a spirit of disillusionment and then disappeared.

Today I ask myself, how did this happen? What became of our lofty plans to use portfolios as an assessment tool to measure our students' growth as writers and our growth as teachers? What happened to the philosophical base we had constructed that guided our decisions about how and why we wanted to establish a four-year portfolio assessment system? Most important, what happened to our desire to be reflective practitioners to improve our teaching and to teach students to be reflective learners to improve their writing?

There are two answers to these questions, the simple one and the complex one. The simple answer I have already alluded to. As the school grew larger, teachers communicated less. Additionally, frequent changes in administrative staff resulted in a lack of informed support. The complex answer is that educational reform cannot be sustained, regardless of how pedagogically sound the practice may be, if new staff members are not acculturated to the beliefs and values that lay behind the establishing of the practice. Stated another way, school reform and those responsible for carrying out these changes need constant attention. We will not bring about change merely by demanding obedience. We cannot expect a group of teachers to buy into a program they do not understand and had no role in creating. In 1992, we were given the chance to welcome new ideas, and we were provided opportunities for growth and rediscovery. Presently, our teachers are given no such opportunity.

So we get the doubts: "Why are we doing this? The kids don't see any value in it! What should I say to them?"

"My kids say they are going to stay home on Senior Showcase Portfolio Day. What should I do? Lower their grades?"

"My kids do a lousy job of reflecting. They just don't know how to do it! Maybe they're too young. Maybe we should rethink why we bother to use portfolios."

Their comments jolt me. As I look in earnest at their faces, it strikes me that we are no longer the same department. These teachers have not read and argued and explored. They have not been asked to bring their experiences to the table. Over the years, the many new teachers who have been hired were told about the portfolio process, but the description was all nuts and bolts; there was no time to discuss philosophy. As we grew from a student body of 1500 to one of 2700, we made serious mistakes that perhaps can serve as a caution to others interested in school reform.

A Look Back

Error #1: We assumed that the newly hired young teachers had learned about the value of portfolio assessment in their teacher education classes. What we ultimately discovered was that they had read about portfolio assessment but felt ill prepared to make decisions about process or design. Unfortunately, we gave this second generation of teachers only a set of operating instructions: "Tell your students to save all written work in this folder. At the end of the year they will pick four pieces and the rest will be taken home. Then they will evaluate these pieces and write a reflective essay about what they have learned this year. The essay will be graded holistically on a six-point scale (see the department chair). At the end of their senior year, they will present their portfolio with sixteen pieces at Senior Showcase Portfolio Day."

Without a firmer base, some of the teachers quietly ignored the rules, hoping they would go away. Their students did not collect work. Therefore, they had nothing to select from at the end of the year. Neither was there anything to reflect on. Our innovation was gradually dying from neglect.

Error #2: We assumed that the acculturation of our new teachers would take place naturally as they learned the system. After all, we shared a large department office. What talk there was, however, centered on questions of "how" instead of "why," and our band of explorers soon became the minority voice, learning a hard lesson along the way: passing along how we do something but not why we do it not only results in uninformed instruction, miscommunication, and lack of motivation, it also limits progress. "Where do we go from here?" is a question that can be answered only by those who know where they have been. With only two remaining English teachers from the original six, we were essentially an English department without a history, with no collective knowledge of the bad old days before portfolio assessment or the struggle to make things better. As far as the new teachers were concerned, portfolio assessment was much ado about nothing. The kids were too immature to reflect meaningfully, their selections had no effect on the curriculum, and if the works were already graded, then the teacher had unwittingly classified the student's work as good, average, or poor writing. Why bother keeping a writing folder? Only now do I see our folly, believing that the new teachers could live our history by rubbing shoulders with us. I see that any reform movement must include an invitation to bring new people on board, a careful plan that works toward inclusion. We had held tightly to our inner circle, believing we were the core, and circled the others around us. All that we lacked were crowns!

Error #3: We assumed that our beliefs were the best because we had come by them through hard work and so invited no discussion and left no room for questions that threatened our system. We explorers had become settlers. We were proud of ourselves, and our pride shut out each new teacher to the department because we saw ourselves as the experts. If we had opened up for change, we feared that new ideas would have rendered ours invalid, old. Perhaps it was our age difference that threatened us, that prevented us from inviting questions about process. Except for Dawn, we were all forty- or fifty-something. We were writing project teacher-consultants. We had master's degrees. The new teachers were in their middle to late twenties. They could be our children.

Our school reform attempt crumbled, but I do not believe aborted efforts at change are unique to our district. In fact, I would argue that in many school districts, whether the change is to portfolio assessment or to some other innovation to improve student learning, the lack of attention to new personnel and the unwillingness to embrace new teachers in continuous grassroots talk will prove fatal for any reform movement. I feel sad that our story typifies many educational reform movements across the nation. "What is *in* this year?" teachers often joke with one another. "New math or old math? Whole language or phonics? Project-based learning or back to basics?" How do we survive the chaos?

In this environment, I have come to believe that the National Writing Project may provide one of the few opportunities for sustained improvement in education. The model provides opportunities for teachers to come together over and over again as they pursue professional growth and allows them to belong to a professional community that sustains and nurtures that growth. In fact, it was at a California Writing Project writing retreat that I began this article, receiving the support I needed to reflect on, and learn from, my experience. The project empowers teachers with their own knowledge and provides a home for the likes of me, an old teacher with a young heart yet one who is never too old to learn, even from failure.

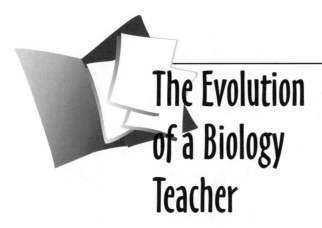

The Evolution of a Biology Teacher

John Dorroh

Using portfolios changes Dorroh from the "old me" to a teacher who finds new ways for his students to become scientists.

For almost twenty-five years, I have been teaching science to high school students, over half of that time in my living lab, Room 202, at West Point High School in West Point, Mississippi. Here I teach biology, perhaps the academic discipline most susceptible to change. Much of the biology that affects our world is embedded in a language that did not exist when I was a beginning teacher in 1976: clones, recombinant DNA, plasmids, gel electrophoresis, and the Human Genome Project, to name a few. As the content of biology has evolved, so have I as a classroom teacher.

Part of my evolution has been learning about portfolios. Since I have been a portfolio devotee for almost ten years, it is time to reflect on this evolution and to remind myself of how and why my classroom environment has changed. What have I learned about the portfolio-writing processes in the last ten years? What was the catalyst for this adventure that today I find as natural as breathing?

Up until 1990, I had had no personal experience with portfolios. I knew that they existed and that a handful of states (Vermont, for example) had tried to use them for statewide assessment. But I thought of a portfolio primarily as a tool for an artist, definitely not one for high school science teachers and students.

Despite this unfamiliarity, in July 1991, I joined about thirty teachers and administrators on the campus of Mississippi State University as a member of the state's task force to incorporate portfolios into the classroom.

I realized that the first question I needed to answer for myself was "Why should I use portfolios?" In what way would a collection of student work, augmented by student reflection on this work, be an improvement over what I had been doing? These questions forced me, perhaps for the first time in my teaching career, to consider some of my basic classroom practices. For instance, I knew after listening to my students for fifteen years that their mastery of content in biology could not be measured exclusively by their performance on multiple-choice tests. To merely give back information was not to think like a scientist. And I wanted students to experience how scientists work, in part to counter the media image of absentminded, wild-haired men with no social lives, totally consumed by their dedication to smoking test tubes. I thought that the use of portfolios might help my students work more like scientists and push them toward a better understanding of science. Further, I wanted students to understand that scientists write, that every stage of scientific work involves getting words down on paper. A collection of science writing would underscore this fact.

But what were these portfolios to look like?

Shortly before I began this adventure, I developed a checklist of portfolio components that would help me gauge how each student had grown as a scientist during the school year. In the process, I took what was for me a big risk: after explaining the nature of portfolios and portfolio assessment, I asked students what they thought should be in the portfolios.

I was surprised when their ideas coincided with many of mine. We honed our collaboration to develop the following official checklist:

1. A composition titled "How I See Myself as a Scientist." This essay I assigned at the beginning of the school year—my first effort to encourage students to think of themselves as scientists. I was, of course, not expecting much. This was a topic that few students had thought about. But by the end of the year, when I asked students to write on the topic "How I *Now* See Myself as a Scientist," they were able to approach the subject with some thoughtfulness and fluency.

2. An essay on some assigned science-related topic. On this one, I fell into the familiar trap of assuming that ten or eleven years of English instruction would make students competent as essay writers. Instead, many had a hard time understanding that an essay is not a report but rather a mesh of opinion and fact.

3. A piece on a biological topic of the student's choice. Students were able to research topics as varied as diabetes, AIDS, and the disappearance of frogs.

4. The best lab write-up. Here, students felt more comfortable; they claimed that this writing was "more like science" than the other writing they were doing. But I wanted them to understand that scientists need to be able to communicate with nonscientists, so I asked them to direct these reports not to me but to some third party.

5. Two best graphs.

6. Two best journal entries. Students usually began each class period by writing for five to seven minutes on some assigned topic related to what we were studying. (See figure 1.)

7. A note-making sample. I introduced students to the use of a double-sided notebook, the left side devoted to traditional note taking and the right side allowing space for questions, opinions, and sketches.

8. A free choice, which allowed students to put their best foot forward.

9/17/96

#8 "All About the Plasma Membrane"

The plasma membrane is selectively permeable. That word sounds like a snobbish girl. The word "selectively" reminds me of someone very picky about what they do and how they look. This is one comparison that sort of makes me understand better. Also, the book described the membrane as a shoe factory. Without materials the shoes can not be made. But, if the factory has too much garbage production will be impossible.

Last week we did an activity on what makes up the membrane. I found it interesting that cholesterol was a part of the membrane. I thought cholesterol was totally bad for you. I learned that I was wrong.

FIGURE 1   A journal entry from a student portfolio

Next, I gave every student a plain manila folder to be used as a collecting file. Each class had its own decorated box in which to store the folders. Everything that I graded, read, or considered in one way or another was returned to the students to be filed by them. (I had enough work to do without having to fret over filing more papers.) Students could also file work I had not seen. I asked students to make selections from their collection files every three to four weeks. We started with the number one item on our checklist and proceeded in order to number eight. Even though my students seemed to be responding positively to the monthly selection process, I still did not know whether I was using the "right" approach. After all, this was not a cookbook approach to evaluation, and I had never seen a high school biology portfolio. There were no models to examine.

I did believe I had made a substantial beginning. But it seemed as if students were merely collecting their work and trying to complete their checklist. They were not thinking like scientists, and they often seemed bored, as if they were filling in blanks on worksheets from their science textbooks. I knew something was amiss, that my checklist might be too restrictive, but for lack of a better idea, I clung to it.

Chad's Influence

That changed after my encounter with Chad. With his red hair, longer than anyone else's in the room, and his Darth Vader T-shirt, covered with his gray flannel shirt, he looked the part of a free spirit, an artist perhaps.

In class, Chad was always doodling.

"I'm listening, Mr. D," he'd say when I brought this behavior to his attention. A fellow teacher told me not to worry, that often students use doodling and sketching to process information; this was news to me. Like so many of my own teachers who had had control of what I did in their classrooms, I felt that doodling went under the broad heading of what they would call "daydreaming" and what educators today might call "being off task."

At a conference with Chad, I paid particular attention to one of his drawings, not a doodle, but one he had handed in to me for my evaluation. Somehow I got the idea that I should push Chad a little further.

"Chad," I began, handing back to him an exquisitely drawn, colored, and labeled picture of a standard cell, "this cell is great. Truly, it is perhaps the best cell I've ever seen a student create. But . . . "

Chad looked away toward the wall, waiting for the inevitable. "Okay," he said, "but what?"

I chose my words carefully. "Even though this cell, as I've said, is a magnificent rendition of a true cell, it lacks something."

"What? What could that cell lack? It's got everything—a nucleus, a cytoplasm, ribosomes; it's got . . . "

"I know, I know," I said. "It does indeed have all of the required parts; however, in all honesty, it's . . . it's . . . it's sort of flat."

I waited.

"Flat, huh? But it's supposed to be flat. . . . It's a paper model."

"You know what I mean, Chad. I know it's a paper model, but you need to advance this project to a higher level. Show me that you understand how all of those parts work."

"Just like that?" asked Chad.

"Yes, just like that. You can do it."

The next day Chad rushed into the classroom, looked at me, and said, "I think you're gonna like it, Mr. D," as he rustled through his pack to retrieve the revised creation. (See figure 2.)

"Here it is. What do you think?" I examined the new cell, not sure at first what improvements had been made.

"This is a futuristic cell," said Chad. He was excited and began to point out the new or modified cell parts. "This is an organelle to help compensate for the depleted ozone layer, and this one . . . "

"I'm impressed, Chad, really impressed. Hand me the old cell so that I can compare the two."

"Is this what you wanted, Mr. D? Is this better? Is this one right?"

All I could say was, "Yes, yes, and yes! We need to talk after I have had some time to study this more carefully and show it off to the other science teachers. Do you mind if I share this?" I asked.

"Be my guest," he said, smiling.

Chad's rendition of the futuristic cell gave me the impetus for taking science "out of the box," allowing students to present what they had learned in various ways. If I was able to see art as a way to let students show what they know, why couldn't I use other activities such as skits and game shows and all forms of creative writing to allow students to showcase their knowledge? The portfolio would remain important, but my checklist would become less important.

I continued to learn and increasingly understand that students differ in their personalities, appetites, attitudes, and modes of learning; and just as each artist's portfolio is different, each student scientist also needs an opportunity for personal expression. I now wanted students to experiment with different techniques for demonstrating they had mastered the material. Portfolios had become a vehicle for allowing them to display their best work in their own "zones," and even though we were still using a checklist, students had much more from which to choose.

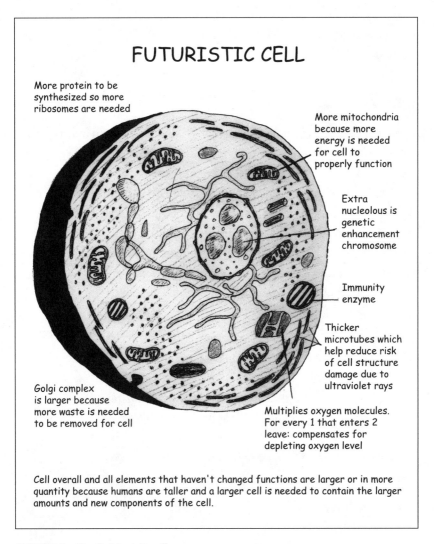

FIGURE 2   Chad's futuristic cell

I decided that if I was going to allow students this kind of freedom, I would need to learn to tolerate—even appreciate—the unorthodox. When a student wrote a lab report in the form of a personal letter to rock star James Hatley, I was not sure that I was thrilled at the prospect of abandoning my age-old, five-part lab write-up, but the students were teaching me invaluable lessons, demonstrating what they could learn beyond information for a test. The portfolio format was helping me give up some control. I became more than a disseminator. Everyone in my classes learned to take risks, including me. My job was becoming more fun.

Becky's Influence

Even so, I had the vague feeling that we needed to go to another level, and it was Becky who showed me the way. "Hey, Mr. D," she asked, "what do we do with these selections once we've chosen them and put them into our portfolio folder? Shouldn't we do something with them?" Becky was right. Up until this point, we had had no element of reflection in our portfolio program. This question led to the development of a self-evaluation sheet, a series of eight questions intended to lead students into analysis of the pieces they had selected. For instance, I asked, "If you had to take this selection one step further, what would you do?"

Reflection was not a skill that came easily to students.

Here is Keith's early-in-the-year reflection on a graph he constructed:

Question: How does this selection allow you to see yourself as a scientist?
Reflection: It lets me see myself taking and graphing data.
Question: How does this selection allow you to see yourself as a better thinker?
Reflection: It gives me more information to process in my memory.

However, later in the year, in April, Keith wrote:

Question: How does this selection (a journal entry on biostatistics) allow you to see yourself as a scientist?

Reflection: Don't all scientists deal with statistics? I know I did! You need to understand statistics so you can decide if the treatment caused a significant change. Scientists use math every day. I did too.

Jan's Influence

I continued to use the portfolio components I had developed for a number of years, feeling comfortable making only minor adjustments in the process. But in the summer of 1997, I met Jan Bergamini from the Bay Area Writing Project, who was a visiting teacher with the National Writing Project Teacher Exchange Program. When I told her about my portfolio checklist, Jan made a radical suggestion: "Why not let students pick whatever they want at selection time rather than sticking to a fixed checklist?" Taking another giant risk, I decided to give this idea a try. I tossed out the checklists and let students select items they felt best demonstrated their strengths. I admit that I did urge them to have a "balanced portfolio" rather than a majority of one-of-a-kind selections. Surprisingly, however, most students saw for themselves that a balanced portfolio gave a more complete picture of themselves as budding scientists.

I learned from this modification that when my students have more ownership and autonomy in the selection process, they take more pride in what they choose to include, and they are more willing to share.

To augment students' growing sense of ownership of their work, I began to urge students to personalize the look of their portfolios. I asked them to extract golden lines from their journals and plaster their cover page with these quotes. A golden line is a sentence or sentences in which a student takes special pride.

I also supplied glue, magazines, markers, pens, and colored pencils to aid students in personalizing their portfolios. I'd taken pictures of students in the lab behaving like professional scientists, mixing chemicals, weighing objects, quizzing fellow students about what ants do in the winter or why worms come to the surface of the ground after a heavy rain. I encouraged them to glue those photos onto the front of their folders as evidence that they were emerging as scientists.

In the last ten years, I've seen how our portfolio program has grown and evolved. What began as a plan to have my students keep their work in manila folders blossomed into a vehicle for opening up my teaching and for allowing students to present in varied ways what they are learning and thinking. Each year we tried something new, developing creative activities for our checklist, adding a reflective component, personalizing our portfolios, and then abandoning checklists in favor of "free" selections.

Through all these changes I held to my original goal: I wanted portfolios that would allow students to see themselves as scientists, to demonstrate, in writing, that they were scientists.

Lessons Learned

What are the "big lessons" I have learned in the past ten years about using portfolios in my science classes?

1. Portfolios soften students' resistance to seeing themselves as scientists. Why? I think that acting as recorders allows students to look at themselves in a kind of intellectual mirror. Sometimes they do not like what they see and they decide to change. Other times they like the mirror's reflection and have reason to celebrate.

2. The atmosphere of the classroom changes when students are making selections. Could it be that this is an act of engagement, one of the most important habits of mind in science? I observed during the selection days that the students' language changed; they were being reflective without realizing it. I liked the atmosphere and recognized the need to do more of it.

3. I learn something new, interesting, and/or exciting about each student from his or her portfolio. Bernie, for example, became our resident greenhouse expert when she extended her love of hands-on experimentation out to the courtyard where the greenhouse and raised beds stood. I didn't know that a teenager could love planting and caring for seeds as much as Bernie did. She took measurements and entered the data into her logbook without

being told to do so, and she encouraged others to do the same. I saw leadership qualities in Bernie that had been masked during the first semester.

4. Portfolios help to pull together lots of pieces. For me, working through my evolving portfolio plan was like assembling a jigsaw puzzle. I wanted students to produce a record that would demonstrate that they were thinking like scientists. I wanted them to connect the work of science with the skill of writing. I wanted them to be free to present what they had learned in a form compatible with their talents, and I wanted them to reflect, select, and take responsibility for their own work.

In the past decade, my teaching style has evolved immensely. One of the biggest triggers of that change was the incorporation of portfolios into the classroom, a decision that changed everything. And as the portfolios evolved over these years, so did the way I see my role as a classroom teacher. That change caused a change in how I managed my classroom. I was now a different and better teacher, and my students were the beneficiaries.

Change, however, is not easy. This has been especially true about my teaching career. Where I used to see problems and obstacles, I now see opportunities to change. In the early years of portfolio involvement I was afraid to try new things. I was learning to give up control of my classroom, to take risks, and to place the responsibility of learning on the shoulders of my students. Simply stated, I had to learn how to trust—how to trust my students, myself, and the portfolio process.

Portfolios helped me to learn how to reflect upon my teaching practices and how to help my students reflect on their learning. I had to learn about logistics—how to orchestrate reasonable deadlines, how to put a numerical grade on works of art, and how to avoid increasing my paper load. Overall, I had to learn how to let the "old me" die and how to keep the new one alive. Portfolios pulled all the little pieces together and helped my students to see themselves as scientists, which was the principle reason I had embarked on this journey in the first place.

Throw Me a Life Jacket: The Portfolio as an Instrument of School Survival

Lisa Piazza

This fourth-year high school teacher turns district-mandated portfolios into insightful collections that students truly value.

had already heard about the flood, but I didn't realize how bad it was until Brenda, the vice principal's secretary, gave me a hug as I entered the office.

"Your room was hit the worst," she said. "I'm sorry. There's not much left to salvage."

It was 1999, the start of my third year teaching English to ethnically and academically diverse ninth-graders at Alameda High School in northern California. My first thought was of the many books I had purchased over the first two years of my teaching career. My second thought was of my students' portfolios and the months of hard work that had gone into creating their collections of best writing. Our school policy asks teachers to store the folders over the summer so the kids don't lose or ruin them, but there I stood, the keeper of one hundred soggy, moldy, definitely ruined portfolios.

I braced myself for my students' disappointment when they returned on exchange day to collect their work from the previous year. It would have been easier to lose if the portfolio were merely a folder stuffed with everything from the previous year. However, what it contained was a compilation of pieces that each student considered his or her best work. Each portfolio had become an individual record for assessment, a valuable collection of work more illustrative of student growth than any standardized test or state-mandated exit exam. Students had created portfolios over the course of the entire school year, and they had spent the last month of that year choosing and reflecting on the material they wished to include.

Our district requires in a portfolio the following items: a short personal and academic résumé, one reflective essay commenting on social and scholarly growth, and one piece of writing from both the beginning and end of the year to use as support for the reflective essay. However, I wanted students to include not only these required specimens but also writing they considered their best work. I have found that allowing kids to decide which pieces they want to keep and label their best produces folders full of creative work and insightful commentary worthy of the Senior Exit Portfolio used as a graduation requirement for the district. In the past, students have been encouraged to take this collection with them to job or college interviews to present as an example of their hard work.

Before the Flood

Standing in my flooded room, I thought back to Vanessa, a bubbly cheerleader in second period who, the previous May, was the first to open her writing folder on portfolio compilation day. She arrived in the classroom to find manila folders stuffed with letters, essays, poetry, vocabulary, stories, and short response papers stacked high on the tables. The folders are usually stored in files at the back of the class with easy access for students, who, at the end of each quarter, must add the work they deem worthy of saving.

"Look at this! September 1—I wrote this on the first day of school," she squealed as she sat down slowly in her chair on compilation day, reading the paper and remembering back to that day many months ago. When she was done, she flipped through the stack to see what was next.

Her classmates soon arrived and quickly found their folders and their seats, creating an atmosphere of jovial reflection. Cedric actually put his enormous sci-fi book down to look at his work, while A.D. eagerly turned to see his favorite independent reading project, the one about the book he actually read, with a grade he likes to see again and again: A+ Excellent.

Their excitement was due partly to the fact that their ninth grade year was finally ending. Looking back and remembering the early days was easy since the work was done and only summer lay ahead.

But the other part of their enthusiasm stemmed from the fact that as they dug through these folders they came across old friends, parts of themselves they had long since forgotten. Shy Derrick revisited his identity poem, which read, "Just because I'm Asian doesn't mean I only use chopsticks / doesn't mean I can't speak English / doesn't mean I don't understand what you say to me."

Samantha relived her experience with unrequited love while reading her character analysis of Romeo Montague. Andrew looked over his personification poem, reading again about winter becoming a shadow of his grizzled grandfather. Justin returned to his own sonnet, a poem good enough to be published in the school newspaper. Sonya giggled over the last line in her acrostic neighborhood poem, a reference to the silly arguments that go on in her house.

All of these assignments combined to reflect a significant portion of their ninth grade year. The pieces told them what they were thinking way back in October and showed them how much they had changed.

So, in September of my third year teaching, I worried about what I could possibly say to them about their ruined folders. I wondered if they would remember these pieces and the lessons learned. Did they need to keep the assignment in order to remember what they had learned from it, or did the fact that they spent time scrutinizing and evaluating their work for the portfolios mean more in the end?

In the spring of the previous school year, at the time of portfolio compilation, I had allowed the festive paper-sorting ambience to permeate the classroom for twenty minutes. I wanted my students to spend time with their work, get reacquainted, and connect on whatever level they were capable of. For some, five minutes was enough. English was not their first language, and every mark was seen as an embarrassment, every spelling correction a reminder of how hard using this language really is. But I allowed time for those students, and I was often surprised to see them peek back in and take another look, hoping to find it was not all so bad. Because, of course, it wasn't.

During this time I walked around the room and looked over their shoulders, curious to see what each was choosing as his or her best. More often than not, I was surprised to discover what the kids considered their premier pieces from the year. This day of sorting and the resulting portfolio of work taught me more about the year than I ever would have imagined. I discovered what assignments they considered worthwhile and which pieces they were proud of, despite the grade and margin marks. I have found that what is kept and what is thrown away says as much about the course and me as it does about the student.

Although they will never admit it, most students, I have learned, enjoy a good challenge. The harder the assignment, the harder they work and the more they treasure the end product. I am continually surprised to see students include in their portfolios work they complained about, lamenting the hours lost from skateboarding and video games. Now, suddenly, this assignment is the pinnacle piece, and they show it off to all. I have also found that my students like to save creative responses to literature, such as writing thematic poems or a series of letters between characters. Some save only vocabulary quizzes, even though I protest and enunciate: "Writing only!" Still, they want to showcase memorization skills and the fact that they can actually use words that once seemed as unreal as nonsense language.

Marcus

I realize the importance of observing and learning from what is included in the portfolio even more when I think back to Marcus, a boy who transferred into my class late in the final semester of that year. He had thrown an empty Snapple bottle at his last unfortunate English teacher and came to me wearing an embarrassed, slightly proud grin and carrying a slew of warning notes from his counselor.

I sat him close to the front in the tiny classroom designated for the new, unsuspecting teacher. His annoyance with English class was clear by the way he slumped into the room each day without any supplies and proclaimed, "We're not doing anything today, are we?" It seemed a daily shock to him that he might need a piece of paper and something to write with.

Naturally, Marcus was stumped when it came to compiling his portfolio. Nothing from his previous teacher had been given to me, so he was stuck with a half-written essay on *Romeo and Juliet*, in which he missed the point completely and received a low D, and an average response paper based on Bebe Moore Campbell's *Sweet Summer*, in which he had to recall the sights and sounds of the summers past. Then there was his "United States of Poetry" poem. He had forgotten it, as ninth grade boys are apt to do.

The poetry assignment had been inspired by the PBS video *The United States of Poetry*. I had filled the end of the year with poetry, knowing that, as the heat of summer fast approaches, nothing but verse will make sense. We are all speaking in metaphors by this time anyway: fear of the unknown sophomore year hides in every spiteful "You don't know that?!" and in every changing body beside my desk clamoring eagerly for answers to questions not yet formed enough to ask.

Because Marcus could not write essays with results higher than a D-, he was leery about the poetry assignment. When he realized he had to write his own poem using a stack of words gathered from the video, he slumped in his chair. He regarded the pile of words on his desk as enemies; they were objects to battle, subjects to force into some kind of meaning that could not possibly make sense to him, or to his teacher, for that matter.

He spent most of the period looking at other people's work, criticizing as only the insecure can do. His classmates ignored him or taunted, "At least I have one. Where's yours?" His head would jolt then, and he'd stare contemptuously at his empty paper.

Toward the middle of the class, I intervened by placing a word in the center of his blank page: one small piece of white paper reading, "here." It was a white flag begging him to surrender to the assignment, waiting for him to spiral into productivity, perhaps even creativity.

He worked quickly, gluing word after word. In the end, the poem was the only thing in his portfolio. The cover letter read, "I now understand that I am a poet. And writing isn't so hard."

As a teacher, I look forward to reading these cover letters more than to seeing the work itself. As I read, I realize again that reflection is primarily for the students' benefit, that by revisiting their work they are able to mark clearly their academic and personal growth. Through this process, they can see their achievements, as Marcus was able to do. He had forgotten about the poem until I reminded him that it could be part of his portfolio. The portfolio gave Marcus a chance to spotlight this work and say out loud, "I am a poet."

Why, then, was I worried about the moldy folders in my flooded room? If the portfolio is truly a beneficial way to teach students about their own learning, then what was important was the process they'd already followed, not the end product. The completed portfolio served to show what students knew and what they still needed to learn at the close of their ninth grade year. Wasn't that knowledge more to the point than the gathering of papers that had brought them to this understanding?

I did not expect the students to see it that way. I prepared myself for the angry look on Marcus's face when he asked for his poem back and Vanessa's eager smile, then quick frown when she realized her folder was gone. When they arrived, they were eager to show off their sophomore status and tell me tales of their summer adventures. Reluctantly, I showed them the mess of their molding folders. Andrew stomped off dejectedly, saying, "Great. Thanks a lot." But some of the others stayed and tried to salvage bits and pieces, pulling out poems and projects, leaving the unrecoverable ones to me.

They knew that keeping their work was a visual reminder of who they were last year and what they knew as ninth-graders. For some, rescuing what little they could meant they will have a physical place for ninth grade in their final portfolio. Either way, I hope the skills learned and reflections recorded will have a permanent place in their minds whether or not the work is present.

Another Flood

Oddly enough, now that I am about to start my fourth year in teaching, I feel as if I've been hit with another flood. Perhaps the soiled, soggy room I began with last year was an omen for what was to come: a deluge of rhetoric about assessment and accountability, state tests and exit exams, rigid grading policies, and my own worries over providing my students the skills needed to make it in a changing society.

Where is the portfolio to fit in all this? This past year, postflood, I felt obligated to dictate what each portfolio should contain, down to order, size, and style. I even went so far as to buy each student the same dark teal folder so each one would look the same. I created a superficial standard for the students to meet in hopes of imbuing seriousness to the project akin to the severity of the hours of multiple-choice testing they endured throughout the year. Absurdly, this somehow made the portfolio seem more legitimate, at least to me, at least at the time.

What had once been an individualized way of assessing growth became prescriptive and standardized, and I fell right into the trap, dragging my students along with me. Gone were the class-time moments of joyful recognition of past assignments and genuine reflection. What I ended up with, instead, were nearly empty folders. The kids were so uninspired by my businesslike approach that most of them were terrified to put their work into something so utterly official looking. They did not approach the portfolio as a collection of past work to be used to assess their own abilities and strengths; it became, instead, a device for someone else to use to judge them, much like a testing Scantron sheet.

As a result, nothing in their writing folder seemed good enough to them; no work could be called "best" by the standard I had set. They supplied the mandatory personal growth essay, a basic evaluation of their skills, and a scant résumé. They found a piece of writing from October and one from May and called the assignment complete. None of them had much to say in their cover letters beyond a simple summary of the assignment. They were asking me what to write, to explain to them what they had learned, so afraid were they of "getting it wrong."

I soon realized that I had flirted with, or more likely fallen into, a lockstep approach to portfolios. As a new teacher, I was intent on giving sanction to my classroom portfolios by surrounding them with mandates, not unlike those I was experiencing from the state and district. I wanted to keep pace, to make our local portfolios something recognizable on a larger stage. What I learned was how this kind of thinking can crash in on a classroom and change a meaningful experience into a useless procedure, leaving in its wake one hundred stunned students holding up virtually empty folders.

This sort of flood proved much more detrimental than the physical one a year earlier. At least those students had been given the opportunity to experience the power of using the portfolio as a hands-on way to understand personally their academic growth and needs. They were given permission to chart their own progress and were allowed the time to revel in their breakthroughs. In contrast to a confidential standardized test, where the questions are long gone by the time the scores arrive, the portfolio process allowed these students to learn openly from their mistakes. The students who participated in the full portfolio experience came to realize that studying and measuring their individual scholastic achievement was crucial to their academic maturity. They understood that the portfolio existed for and belonged to them much more than it belonged to the district or teacher.

In this age of exit exams and accountability, where schools and teachers profit or lose from the scores of their students, it will be a struggle to hold on to the integrity of such a valuable assignment as the portfolio. If students now need to pass only one test to graduate, what will become of the process for allowing students to study their own development? After all, a test score is only one number; the portfolio, a collection of information and thoughtful rumination, can be the life jacket that holds them afloat in the testing tsunami.

What We Write About When We Write About Love

Jane Juska

Jane Juska finds portfolios as indispensable to her teaching inside the walls of San Quentin State Prison as they were in her high school classroom.

Lefty's portfolio is a sight to behold. It is beautiful. Somewhere he has gotten a blue folder and the use of a word processor. Each of the four pieces he has selected, along with their drafts and cover notes, rests in its separate file folder inside the blue cover. The course label on the cover, for which the portfolio is a major assignment, looks like this:

Bryan ————
English 234: Literary Genres
READING, WRITING, AND TELLING STORIES
Spring 2000
Final Assignment: English 234 Portfolios
Instructor: Jane Juska
San Quentin State Prison

Not all of the fifteen portfolios my students at the prison handed to me on the final night of class were beautiful. Some were simply lined pieces of paper held together with a paper clip, a paper clip being a difficult thing to get and the source of which I do not question any more than I query Lefty, a.k.a. Bryan, on his access to materials. Some of the pieces in some of the portfolios are written in pencil. Pens are available in the prison store but are expensive, given that the average pay for these men and their forty-hour workweek is seventeen cents an hour. No matter the roughness of the portfolios, every single one of them comes in. "I just want you to know," says Steve, handing me his portfolio, "a lot of work went into this." His smile, invisible for a good part of the semester, is pleased, proud. Lots of smiles this final night, smiles of relief, of pride, of gratitude to the college program, to me. I will get fifteen hugs of varying intensity at the end of class and will find fifteen love letters of varying intensity in their portfolios. At home, reading and responding to their selections, to their "Dear Reader" letters, to their cover notes, their drafts, their starters, I will write love letters back, slip them into the portfolios, and one week later return them to the prison.

My clearance still being good, I will enter the three checkpoints, be wanded, stamped, questioned, and finally let in to the quadrangle of the prison itself. On my left is a building called the Adjustment Center. It is the Hole. Behind the Hole is Condemned Row. It is Death Row. On my right is the chapel, and in front of me is my destination, the Education department. It is here I deposit the portfolios and am promised their safe return to their owners. It is likely I will never see my students or their portfolios again.

Over the five semesters I have taught English 234 at San Quentin State Prison, my students have been a teacher's dream. My course is an elective, a good start in a system where precious little is elective. While the vast majority of men in prison read below sixth grade level, my students—most of them lifers—have high school diplomas or GEDs. Some have college degrees; one or two have Ph.D.s. These men are the intellectual crème de la crème of the prison. They have passed an entrance exam, a writing sample composed and scored by me (ah, the pleasure of efficiency in the absence of committees). Right away, you can see teaching such a course is duck soup.

My course—and I say "my" course because I made it up and nobody but me teaches it—is called "Reading, Writing, and Telling Stories." It is part of the Patten College Program, Patten College being a small evangelical college that, as part of its community outreach, does the business of registration and transcripts. The men can earn their AA degree, and so far, sixteen of them have. The instructors come from the Berkeley and Davis campuses of the University of California; the teaching assistants are graduate students and wonderful. I come from St. Mary's College, which, it is hoped, will underwrite a four-year degree program in the near future.

We don't get paid. We don't get any books; we have to hustle them ourselves. We don't get appreciated by the guards because we make more work for them (all those extra movements of all those prisoners). And then, of course, there's the matter of fear.

"Were you afraid to come here?" David asked one night during class.

"No," I said, "I used to teach high school." My remark brought down the house, for, in the midst of our laughter, we all knew that there were those among us who, on occasion, might have made the classroom less than secure. Now, they are grown, these men. Here in San Quentin, the students are achingly polite, desperate to reclaim manners they never had or never refined, desperate to reacquaint themselves with their own humanity.

Most of my students have been in prison more than twenty years; many of them have little or no hope of getting out. Eddie is thirty-four, incarcerated since he was eighteen; over the course of several semesters, he will become a poet. Randy, whose age remains a mystery, has been incarcerated for forty-two years; on the last night of the semester, he will hold us spellbound when he reads from his portfolio the story of his life: "My mama [his mama stabbed his father to death in front of four-year-old Randy] never let me go hungry and always entertained her visitors on the other side of the curtain." At the end, he will look at all of us, at me, and say, "Just you remember what my mama told me, 'Good-bye don't mean gone.'"

What, then, makes a good writing course for men whose self-respect is low, whose intelligence is high, whose self-confidence is absent, whose education is spotty or long past, whose daily life is one of unremitting dullness save for frequent incidents of violence, whose constant companion is despair? What's the best way to prove to them they can write? Portfolios, that's what. "Let the sun shine in!"

Introducing Portfolios

The course outline, which opens the semester and which I read aloud to the class, includes the following:

Students will create a portfolio of their work derived from classwork, class discussion, and the readings from the assigned text. That portfolio will be submitted to the instructor at the final class meeting. Each student will choose at least one finished piece from his portfolio to submit for publication in a journal or magazine.

The stillness is deafening. What it means is that my students don't understand one thing I have read aloud to them. They are not about to admit in front of the other inmates that they have no idea what to do, that they never heard the word *portfolio*, and that the requirement to submit a piece for publication, while clear enough, is ridiculous. They cannot render into speech "I'm not going to do that." But that's okay. Once we start writing lots of stuff, they will see the possibilities for selecting and submitting.

"Any questions?" I ask. Silence is still king.

Later in the semester, in a clarification, I will write to them the following:

The reflection a writer does is often as important to his growth as the fiction he writes. Therefore, I will look carefully at what you say about each of your packets. [I have mandated a minimum of four.] I will look most carefully at your introductory letter, which you will place at the very beginning of the portfolio. I offer you, by way of example, the "Dear Reader" letter from my own portfolio. Your own "Dear Reader" letter will explain what your readers can expect to find as they move through your portfolio. It will tell us—as the portfolio will show us— who you are. Who you are as a reader/writer/thinker may be different from who you were at the beginning of this course. If so, explain those differences in this letter. Where you are going as a reader/writer/thinker might form a part of this letter. What you are most proud of might show up in the letter; what your concerns are for your future as a writer/reader might appear as well. The final portfolio is not to exceed fifty pages.

By this time, the men feel freer to express their thoughts, yet they are still incredulous. "Fifty pages?! You've got to be kidding!"

"No, no," I reassure them, "*not more* than fifty pages." And although I show them my hastily contrived portfolio, there is no visible lessening of tension.

Throughout the semester they worry. They complain politely: "I'm sorry, Professor"—I'm not a professor, and they know it, but they want me to be, so I am—"but I don't think one semester is long enough to get anything together worth submitting to anybody."

And from a small, sweet voice in the back of the room, "What happens if we don't?"

"I don't know," I say. "Nobody ever hasn't."

They do it. And, though I have not had the pleasure of seeing most of them again, I suspect strongly, I know absolutely, that these portfolios were and are, in various ways, useful. Listen to Frank. He told me this story: "I went before the parole board, and for some reason, I had my portfolio with me with that nice letter you wrote to me about it. And for some reason, I left the portfolio in that room. And when I went back to get it, it wasn't there. And I'm getting out. Now, I can't say for sure. . . ." Yes you can, Frank. Go ahead, say it. You're a free man.

Responding to Portfolios

Reading and responding to portfolios is work. But, unlike too much of the work teachers are expected to do, this is good work. During the years I taught high school, I took sick days to read and respond to my portfolios. I ended thirty-five years of teaching with minus-eight sick days; you can bet they docked me. But so what? By then, I was so convinced of the importance of portfolios I couldn't teach without them. And I still can't. Of all the strategies and techniques I learned and experimented with throughout my career, none had the staying power of portfolios. Only portfolios made sense of what my students and I had been through together; in fact, only portfolios showed my students and me that indeed we had been through a lot together, and here it is now collected and selected and reflected upon. Don't tell me we didn't do anything in here. With portfolios, the evidence of hard work and talent over the long haul was abundant.

For my prisoners, for whom the long haul is possibly forever, portfolios give importance to everything they write. "Throw nothing away!" I remind them again and again. "You won't know 'til later if you want to include it in your portfolio." Still not clear exactly what this portfolio thing is, they nonetheless obey.

On the night we set aside for selecting what will end up in the portfolio, I sit beside Leonard, who is leafing through many, many papers. He asks me, "What do you think about this one?"

I answer, "I like it. Where did it come from?"

Leonard reaches into his shirt pocket and pulls out a few scraps of paper. "From that starter you gave us. And then I made it bigger." He shows me his first and second drafts.

I ask, "What are all these notes and questions?"

"My cellie wrote those," said Leonard. "I show him my writing."

"Pay attention to your cellie," I say. "He's a smart guy."

Leonard smiles. "I'm lucky."

With this kind of evidence—where the piece came from and where the writer took it, how the writer got it there and why; in short, the kind of reflection demanded by the portfolio—the men gain confidence and fluency. This, in an environment where language is monosyllabic and obscene, is nothing short of miraculous.

For men in prison the portfolio takes on an additional importance. In prison they do not own things. Oh, tobacco, which they use to barter for stamps, books from the library, perhaps. But they have no testament to their existence, to themselves as individuals, as men who can do good work. Now they do. The portfolio belongs to them as nothing else can, and it doesn't hurt one bit that the letter from their teacher is warm with praise and encouragement, along with suggestions for further writing and revision and sending stuff out, and now go and do it. Get busy, I urge them. Some of them do, though I will never know for certain.

I have constructed this fantasy. My students, consigned once more to their four-by-five-foot cells and to their cellmates, who may or may not be sympathetic to writing as a reasonable way to spend one's time, sit on their bunks, the light from the bare bulb barely enough to illuminate what my writers have before them. My writers are writing; they are looking at their portfolios, back to my letter; they are revising; they are rereading the addresses of publications they copied out of *Writer's Market* during the semester. Whether they're in North Block (maximum security), H Unit (medium security), or the Ranch (minimum security); whether or not their cellmates encourage their efforts, they are writing. And when things get particularly tough, as they are sure to do, my prisoners will turn to paper and pencil. Dostoevsky, who knew something about prison, wrote, "Every man must have a place to go." My writers have a place.

So yes, reading and responding to portfolios is hard work. And of course, reading and responding to fifteen portfolios beats writing back to seventy or a hundred fifty. The intensity, though, is the same. It is me, closeted in my study, chained to my computer, "getting with" my writers, talking back to them, arguing gently with them, asking questions, and, yes, loving them and telling them so.

Portfolios Speak for Themselves

For his portfolio, Mike has selected his response to Carolyn Ferrell's wonderful story, "A Proper Library," and has combined it with a memory piece:

> *"They slip in and slide out." That was the saying back home about White Castle hamburgers. . . . In this story, there is much said about love. Here in prison, "bone-yards" (conjugal visits) used to be fun. But I agree with Ms. Ferrell, "A few minutes isn't love" and she concludes with "She never knew what love was, man, bitch." Bar-hopping all night long, drunk, tired, and broke, White Castle's was an oasis, . . . back home in Chicago. I rush, speed, and bump into an island or two getting there. If reading is a drug, Carolyn Ferrell had me under the influence.*

King Luther Martin includes a monologue, written in response to an assignment on technique. Here is a part:

Why do you think I go to some funky ass truck school? You think I'd be doing all this if I didn't love you? You know I was just mad, baby. Guess I was tripping, huh? And I'm gonna try to smoke less until I quit.

Adam never quite got over what he saw as the brilliance of his first, introductory letter to me, so he includes it in his portfolio. In it he introduces himself as a painter, movie grip, music clerk, arcade worker, drug dealer, pimp, software engineer, and an inmate worker at San Quentin State Prison. He offers an early history:

Since the fourth grade I have despised the formal education system employed in this country. That was the year I stopped attending public school. With an I.Q. of 172, I terrorized authority figures. Employing a completely rational approach to their 'rules,' I calculated risk/effort versus reward and acted accordingly. Suffice it to say, I was virtually uncontrollable. I drove them nuts.

Adam is twenty-one.

Dennis writes of how he learned to read in Jamaica in the fourth grade:

And she squeezed me and she squeezed me, and I said "O, Miss Mary, don't squeeze so hard!" And she said, "I'm not letting go of you until you read." And she kept on squeezing till I was almost out of breath! I looked up and there was a sign Miss Mary had written on the blackboard. The words came out of my mouth—NO BACKTALK—and Miss Mary let me go. And that's how I learned to read.

Sometimes the writing is so damn good you want to weep. From Steve:

... three and a half months later I found myself in a big, brand new Mercury Marquis, with a good-hustling, strong, fine young fox by my side. The Stones were blasting and I had a hand full of her inner thigh, all hot and silky-smooth and we drove over the George Washington Bridge.... A strong wind was blowing West from the pitch-black of the Atlantic Ocean. Then for the first time, I saw the lights and the giant

skyline of the biggest, baddest City in the U. S. I was twenty years old, my girl was eighteen, and I felt as if I had come home.

The "Dear Reader" letters overwhelm. From John:

"I must admit that I am not an avid writer by any means. . . . I have no stories to tell. . . ." This is but an example of what I wrote in my intro-ductory letter to you. I enrolled in this class out of pure boredom, as a means to break up the monotony of doing time in a 4 x 5 foot cell. . . . I have since gained wisdom. . . . Writing short stories is hard work, and never have I been more committed, or more honest with myself than I have with my readers. I am a writer!

Writing stories has sometimes been more difficult than the rigors of prison life I have faced for over 20 years. Yet, writing has also become a fulfillment. I have gained a new form of expression and free-dom that cannot be quenched. My portfolio is an extension of me— my writing. My stories are a reflection of my life, who I was as a child, where I am today.

Is it any wonder I begin my letter to him, "Oh, John. I hope I get through your portfolio without dampening your pieces."

From Lefty:

Having spent exactly half of my life in prison (uninterrupted), I think, feel, and now am beginning to understand why I want to write. . . . My work is from the heart, it means to me growth, maturity, hope, family, and a desire to put my life in a perspective that is meaningful, thereby negating the circumstance in which I have found myself. I present this work to you, but it is ultimately for me. It is nurturing. It is how I think, what I like to hear and read. And now it is what I write! Before this course, I didn't know that. I didn't feel the need to bleed (that is, bleed ink). I now stand on a platform and I will decide what direction this new writer will take, look, think, feel, tell. . . . !!!

Wynton tells me a secret: "My alias in high school was and still is Em-peror. My teacher said I resembled a younger Haile Selassie I, Emperor of Ethiopia."

William's is short: "Thank you, precious woman. I've learned more than I can now perceive."

As I said, portfolios are all about love.

References

Ferrell, C. 1997. *Don't Erase Me: Stories.* Boston: Houghton Mifflin.

The Teacher's Role in Portfolio Assessment

Joni Chancer

A California teacher finds the role of teachers crucial to the success of student-owned portfolios. She highlights specific classroom practices that prepare students to select and reflect successfully on their writing and reading.

"If portfolios are about self-selection of representative pieces of writing and reflection that only the student can do, then doesn't it follow that the teacher's role in this type of assessment should be minimal?"

As a teacher-consultant of the California Writing Project, I am frequently asked this question by teachers who are interested in changing the way they assess their student-owned portfolio assessment. I was challenged by this same question when I first began using portfolios with my students.

I first heard about portfolios at a conference on assessment held in Los Angeles ten years ago. It was called "Beyond the Bubble," and it brought the issues of assessment out of the closet and into the center of educational research and discussion. I particularly recall one session in which Dennie Palmer Wolf described the portfolios developed by students of art, music, and writing classes as part of a university-based research project. I was especially struck by her closing statement, which I scribbled into my notebook and underlined three times: "The portfolio is more than a collection of work; it is a conscious statement of growth." That statement must be made by the student, but it is a statement that can be supported and enhanced by an ongoing writing and reading program in which the teacher has an active, essential role as designer, facilitator, coach, and researcher. I don't just stand on the sidelines. I teach.

Using portfolios with my students has changed the way I teach. I have learned to become an observer, to take notes and reflect, to view my teaching as my own personal portfolio to revise and refine. I have discovered that, although reflection and the selection of the contents of the portfolio certainly belong to my students, reflection can be taught. It works proportionally: the more ownership I give my student in self-assessment, the more critical my role becomes. It is the teacher who sets in place the conditions and the structures for what will eventually become a portfolio culture.

In this article, I will share the classroom practices I have experimented with and refined in my personal continuing research project. The students I describe are fourth, fifth, and sixth grade students from two schools: Oak Hills Elementary School in Agoura, California, and Las Colinas School in Camarillo, California. Both schools are in suburban residential areas about forty-five miles northwest of Los Angeles. While there is no single dominant second-language group, nearly one-fifth of my students at Oak Hills Elementary are from Middle Eastern, Asian, or Pacific Island countries. Our parent community cares very much about grades, achievement, and the high expectations required for eventual admittance to a university. The spirit of portfolios required something of a shift in attitudes about learning and growth. This was growth that could not be captured in a single grade or in a single score. The final collection, selections, and reflections of the students, as evidenced by the portfolios, convinced the parents of the value of this type of assessment more than any of my words. What blossomed by the end of the year began in September as carefully planted and gradually nurtured seeds.

Starting with Mini-Lessons: Purposeful Play

One purpose of portfolios is to give students an opportunity or a context for reflection and self-assessment. As part of the reflective process, they frequently consider such questions as:

- Why did I write this piece?

- Where did I get my ideas?

- Who is the audience, and how did that affect the piece?

- Was this piece (or parts of it) easy to write? Why?

- Was this piece (or parts of it) difficult to write? Why?

- What parts flowed, and what parts took more time?

- What parts did I rework? What were my revisions?

- If I received response, what was it? What did others like about my piece? What suggestions did they make?

- What am I most satisfied with in this piece, and/or not satisfied with in this piece?

- What skills did I work on in this piece?

- Did I try something new?

- What elements of a writer's craft enhanced my story?

- What might I change? How does this compare to other pieces I have written?

- Do I have a "style" that typically characterizes my writing, and does this piece reflect that style?

- Did something I read influence my writing?

- Is this piece representative of a particular genre or type of writing? What attributes of the genre are reflected in this piece?

- What did I learn, or what will the reader learn?

- What do I want the reader to know about this piece?

- Where will I go from here? Will I publish it? Share it? Expand it? Toss it? File it?

I can't imagine a student answering all these questions about any one piece. Neither are these questions meant to constitute a reflection checklist. However, these questions do seem to be addressed frequently by my students when they tell the story of a particular piece.

For example, Maria (a sixth grade student) included in her portfolio a story titled "No Final Good-bye":

No Final Good-bye

My mother's illness began during an undiagnosed case of rheumatic fever. Her family didn't recognize the signs of the fever because her brother had just died in a boating accident. They thought she was just faking her illness to get some attention.

The lack of treatment for the fever resulted in serious damage to the heart. The doctor's prediction for a normal life was grim. They told her that she would not live past 20 and certainly not have any children.

But she defied their predictions and became a successful business woman, married, had my older brother and me and was a great housewife.

Gradually, after all these years, her heart began to fail.

I really wasn't aware of how serious her condition was, but I knew there was something wrong with my mother that no one was telling me or wanted me to know. I didn't want to go any place with my friends or go to school because I thought she would be gone when I got home. I cried at night knowing she wouldn't be alive and well much longer.

At this time it was near Thanksgiving and everyone in my family was in sort of a fake happiness. Sort of like a false front on an old store; something to cover up the real thing.

Right before Thanksgiving my mother flew back East to a famous heart clinic. The doctors told her of an experimental operation to have new valves put in her heart. But she came back depressed and her hopes for a normal life shattered after the doctors at the clinic told her that she was too old for the operation. She was forty-three and the cut-off age was thirty-nine.

For me the time while she was away was torture. I kept telling myself that my mother would come back and not have to worry about her heart ever again. But then a little voice inside my head told me to face the facts and deal with whatever came up.

Thanksgiving Day my mother went to the hospital and came back, only to have more medicine to take. The doctors could do nothing for her. But even though she had the medicine, she grew weaker. My fears were becoming reality.

I tried to deny what was happening because it was easier to just forget about it. I just wanted to believe that she would jump up and be well again for the rest of her life, just as she had been before. I wanted everything to be back to normal.

Several days before Christmas, I woke up in the middle of the night to the concerned voice of my father calling the doctor. A few minutes later I was downstairs watching the ambulance attendants place my mother on a stretcher. I stood there watching the tail lights of the ambulance fade into the darkened road. I never saw my mother alive again.

The next morning my father woke me and told me that my mother had died at the hospital, in her sleep, without pain.

"No" I screamed. "She can't be dead! They probably got the wrong people mixed up!"

"She's dead," my father said and walked out of the room.

The funeral was the next day. I dreaded the thought of seeing the casket being lowered into the ground.

When my family got to the funeral home, I went right over to the casket and looked in. There my mother lay in her best silk dress, with her face and hands chalk white. I reached to pick her hand up, but dropped it, feeling it was ice cold.

This was truly our final good-bye.   —Maria (sixth grade)

In her letter introducing her portfolio, Maria shares the following story and reflection about the piece with her readers:

'No Final Good-bye' is a true story, and I surprised my writing group with it. It is the story of a girl whose mother dies from heart disease. It is written in the first person, so some of the kids thought it was about me. Well, my mother is still alive! But they thought the story was really

*sad and some of them even started to cry when I read it. When I was
done reading the story to them they didn't want to respond. They said
they were too sad, but I wanted them to tell me what they thought I
had done a good job of in the story. I told them the story was written
about my grandmother, told from my mother's point of view. I inter-
viewed my mom, and then she told the story as if she were writing it
when she was my age. The next day they gave me response. Everyone
liked the metaphors and similes in my story and how I used them to
show my feelings. Mrs. Chancer liked the transitions and the pacing. I
liked how I used the point of view of my mother and convinced my
writing group this was real.*

It is clear that Maria is a writer refining her craft. She knows how
similes and metaphors can make her writing more interesting. She
knows the emotional power of writing and how to sequence and pace
the retelling of events to capture a reader's empathy. She made conscious choices about the point of view and recognized the effect of writing with voice. And yet in the beginning of the year, her reflections
focused on her "neat cursive" and "excellent spelling" and the length of
her stories. What made the difference? I observed that Maria's reflections became richer, more meaningful, and more specific as she was
gradually introduced to elements of the writer's craft.

Throughout the year, a focus of our writing workshop is to play with
these various craft techniques, and mini-lessons have allowed the play to
become purposeful. The design and teaching of the mini-lesson are the
aspects of my writing and reading program in which I feel the most creative and effective. Working with students during craft mini-lessons is
like guiding artists in a studio. The chapter devoted to mini-lessons in
books by Donald Graves, Lucy Calkins, Nancie Atwell, and Rebekah Caplan make a significant difference in my own writing and in the writing of
my students. I recommend the books of these authors to any teachers
interested in designing or refining a classroom writing workshop.

Typically, a mini-lesson in my class begins with the sharing of literature: excerpts from favorite books, lines of poems, favorite dialogue,
interesting character descriptions, even provocative titles and first lines

of novels. For example, one such mini-lesson on dialogue might begin with a quick reader's theater from Judy Blume's *Tales of a Fourth Grade Nothing*, a book filled with humorous, engaging conversation. After the reading, we talk about what Judy Blume did that captured us as readers. The children respond with comments such as these:

"She writes like kids really talk."

"She doesn't use the word said over and over. She uses different words."

"Sometimes the sentences are really short or not even complete, and another character breaks in with a line."

"She tells you what the characters are doing while they are talking so you can imagine it in your mind."

"Sometimes she tells you what the characters say and what they are thinking."

Before the mini-lesson begins, I think about dialogue myself and jot down a few notes. If the children have trouble getting started in their observations, I ask them to look at a particular line, passage, or even a word. I don't tell them what to think, I just focus their attention. As they make their observations, I record them on an overhead. Donald Graves (1991) suggests saving the overheads for future reference. I have found it to be an invaluable suggestion and frequently find myself saying things like, "Remember when we talked about dialogue and you said sometimes the author lets you know what a character says and then what the character thinks? Let's look at what you discovered about dialogue again." The overhead goes up. "Now I'll read a passage from Christopher's story. Tell me if you hear places where his dialogue is really working. The things we record on the overhead might help you."

Along with saving overheads, the children and I save excerpts from their pieces or nominate entire pieces of writing that are good demonstrations of a writer's craft. I use these excerpts over and over in subsequent years. The children look through our "Writer's Craft" binder with pride and see examples of their writing alongside passages from published authors of the literature we read together and individually.

Mini-lessons engage children in listening, focusing attention, learning about writing through connections with reading, experimenting, sharing, and refining. These are the attitudes and activities that eventually foster reflection in the portfolio.

Teaching Reflection: Translating to "Student-Speak"

With the recent emphasis on authentic assessments, we as teachers have been introduced to a new vocabulary. Grade books are no longer at the heart of evaluation. We converse with one another about a child's developing fluency, confidence, and experience as a reader and a writer; we understand what these terms imply. They represent important considerations in the evaluation of our students. The conversation, however, should not be limited to teachers. Ideally, I want my students to be able to reflect upon their self-perceived growth. Beginning in the first week of school, the children and I consider elements of fluency, confidence, and experience, translated into "student-speak." The focus is never negative but encourages honest recognition of strengths, areas to work on, and subsequent goal setting.

Fluency is a topic in our initial discussions and mini-lessons. Many children believe they should read and write effortlessly if they are "really good at it." They are often surprised and relieved to acknowledge that while they may be fluent readers of particular types of books, certain types of books (textbooks, information books, or even poetry) may require more attention and slower-paced concentration; maybe even two or three readings. As an example, I share with my students how I must read computer software instruction manuals slowly, sometimes even orally, before the message clicks and I truly comprehend the information. Sometimes, I need to read the first paragraph or page of a book a few times before I connect with the story and subsequently go on to read with more speed and fluency. I often choose to read poems two or three times, and somehow the meaning becomes clearer with each reading. Before long, the children begin to share examples of instances when they read and write effortlessly and other times when they need to slow down and "work a little harder."

This is a significant breakthrough for many of my students. Never before have they considered their own personal patterns of literacy. The discussions open the door not just to reflection, but also to strategies for learning and personal goal setting. Children learn not to be easily discouraged. This does not mean that they are poor readers. Understanding and accepting this opens the door for some children to what Frank Smith (1988) calls "the club of literacy." Until that door is opened, these students may stay outside the circle of the literate community and resist any consideration of goal setting or reflection of strengths and areas to work on, as this sample demonstrates:

> *I guess I read kind of slowly, at least slower than a lot of other kids. I read a few pages and then I stop and think about what I read, and what the setting is, and I try to get into the book. It works for me and it's just the way I read.*   —Brian (sixth grade)

For other readers, their awareness of fluency patterns indicates their growing maturity and development. We talk about how more experienced and reflective readers sense and acknowledge the different ways they read:

> *When I read the* Doll Hospital *I read it quickly. The vocabulary wasn't difficult and the print wasn't small. The plot was easy to understand. But sometimes I reread a book when the author changes settings quickly, or if the book has harder vocabulary, like in* Harriet the Spy. *Then I take a little longer.*   —Amanda (fifth grade)

> *I sometimes have to read a page over when a book starts off with a lot of characters, like in* Anne of Green Gables *or* The Witch of Blackbird Pond. *Another time when I sometimes slow down my reading or reread parts is when the author uses words I don't understand, like the old-fashioned words in* Little Women.   —Jessica (fifth grade)

> *The books I breeze through are the funny and humorous books, for example Roald Dahl and Judy Blum books. Especially* Matilda! *They have lots of dialogue and I think that makes them easy and fun to read.*   —Brendan (fifth grade)

Fluency in writing is also a topic for discussion from the very first day. As we spend time together in writing workshop, I invite my students to consider if they are writing longer stories. Perhaps it is easier for them to write in a particular genre or style. Are they noticing that they are writing faster? Is it easier to get the words down on their paper? Do they know what to say and how to get started?

Our conversation generally brings us to a consideration of strategies they may want to try. Some find it helpful to talk about a story before they begin to write. Other students cluster their ideas in webs on their paper. Some of my students find it easier to compose on the computer; others seek a quiet place and a familiar notebook or journal.

We talk about spelling and writing in cursive versus manuscript and what to do when either of these considerations becomes a roadblock. We discuss why fluency is important to writing and how personal expectations for first draft perfection can get in the way. Eventually, the discussions come around to the value and freedom that revision brings to the process of writing. Knowing that they can add things to their stories after receiving response or rereading a piece, reorganizing their thoughts on paper, scratching out words or whole sections, explaining things more, and polishing up certain descriptions give students faith that they can jot down ideas for fluency first, and refinement and form can follow.

Eventually, fluency becomes an important focus in portfolio reflections. In their introductory letters to their portfolios, students frequently comment on their fluency as both writers and readers, as these two examples show:

> I think I'm a very good writer. When I write I sit down and the ideas just come to me! It's easy for me to write. When I write you will see I write with detail and description. You can picture it in your mind! My writing is humorous and adventurous. When I write it takes me into another world. I have written all kinds of stories. Mysteries, reports, fantasy, letters, eassys [essays], personal times, anything! No matter if it's an eassy or biografy I include humor, or something to make it interesting and sound like me! I like writing true stories the most because they are easier to write about. I think I'm a much better

writer this year than I was last year and I think the Cree Indian Naming Poem I wrote tells a lot about me.

Writes Like the Wind

Her name tells of how it was with her.
It was then, September of 1991,
that she knew,
she must be a writer.
Her pencil just moved across the paper, magically.
She wrote with creativity and humor.
The words flowed like wind out of her head
and onto the paper.
When she was done,
she was satisfied with her work.
*She had **Written Like the Wind.***

—Lauren

I am a good writer and I am fluent once I have an idea. Sometimes it is hard for me to think of what I will write about. The genre studies we did in writing and reading helped me learn new ways to write this year. It was easier to plan my stories and then my ideas flowed better. My favorite stories that I wrote were: Blue Boy Is Missing, a mystery story; Stephanie and the Magical Book, a fantasy; and The Curse of the Swan, a fairy tale. I like writing fairly tales, fantasy stories and mysteries the most. I have improved as a writer by becoming more descriptive. A goal I have for next year is to write a good adventure story.

—Elizabeth

Both students clearly recognize how considerations of fluency affect their process as writers and readers.

Using Conversation: Reflection in Reading

In December of the first year that I used portfolios with my students, I asked them to "reflect on their personal growth in reading." Not surprisingly, many children responded with uncertainty and puzzled expressions. I quickly figured out that the question was too general and abstract and needed to be broken down into considerations the children would find more meaningful. I also recognized we needed a context or setting for ongoing conversations about books and reading. I wanted the reflections to be a natural part of an ongoing process, not the point of the discussions.

I stumbled into what has become a favorite part of our portfolio classroom—book clubs. I told a teacher friend that I wanted to capture the elements of my adult book club: the sharing, excitement, and anticipation of discovering really good books. I know how powerfully influenced I am by someone else's enthusiastic endorsement of a particular book or author. Nancie Atwell, in her book *In the Middle: New Understandings About Writing, Reading, and Learning* (1987), beautifully describes a structure for sharing self-selected books: reading workshop. My book clubs are a slightly modified spin-off of Atwell's model.

With my fourth and fifth grade students, an equal emphasis is placed upon the oral conversations about books after sharing Lit Letters in an established group. I meet with my students every week in small book clubs of five to seven heterogeneously grouped students. Each club member comes to the meeting with a Lit Letter about a self-selected book. I encourage the children to consider in their letters questions such as:

- What is the title/author/genre/setting/number of pages?
- Why did you choose this book?
- Briefly, what is the book about?
- Who are the characters? What are they like? Do they change?
- Why might someone else want to read this book?
- Does this book remind you of other books you have read?
- What is your overall feeling about this book?
- Did you learn anything from this book? What?
- What is your favorite part?
- What will you remember most about this book?

- Do you have favorite lines or quotes from the book?

- Was this book easy? Difficult? Challenging? Just about right? Why?

The questions focus not just on comprehension, but also on more affective, personal considerations that reflect their processes as readers. Few children answer all the questions, and some children choose not to address them at all. Often, however, the letters seem to be loosely structured according to these considerations, as this letter demonstrates:

Dear club Members,

I just finished a book called Streams To the River, River to the Sea. *It's author is Scott O'Dell. It's genre is Historical fiction. Its through the Lewis and Clark expedition and has 163 pages.*

I chose this book because everybody in my book club read it and said it had wild adventure and true love.

Briefly the book is about a Shoshone girl who got captured by attack. The Minnetarees who captured her betted on her to marry a cruel trader who came often to trade. Charbonneau was his name. Sacagawea was her real name and she had to marry the man without even knowing him. She and her husband join with Lewis and Clark. They needed Sacagawea to show them the way through her hometown which was jagged and hard to climb.

The characters are Sacagawea who is a brave Indian girl with lots of troubles. Captain Lewis, a rugged man with his brain as a compass and Captain Clark a strong man who knows what's best for his crew and others.

No they do not change.

My overall feeling for the book is high thanks to the description in the book and the quality of adventure.

I will remember when Sacagawea got captured it was so sad.

This book was challenging to read because of the strange names like Charbonneau.

Sincerely,
Young (grade four)

Children clearly address their letters to each other, not to the teacher. The other club members then jump off from the letter to a lively conversation. Frequently, students jot down the titles of books that interest them, and I often ask the children to come prepared with a favorite excerpt to read aloud.

Motivation, comprehension, and attention to the process of reading are evident in every letter and group conversation. One of our most memorable discussions focused on a statement one club member made that "Gary Paulson's book *Hatchet* is a boy's book." What followed was an animated conversation that bordered on debate concerning the question of whether a particular book could be gendered. I smiled, remembering how my adult book club argued about the exact same issue.

The book club meeting becomes the context for authentic assessments, providing me with rich opportunities for observation and informal note taking. Frequently during these meetings, I ask questions in student-speak that break down the more abstract query of "How have you grown or developed as a reader?" When responding to these questions, the children discuss with each other

- if they are reading longer books, "chapter" books, or if they are reading for longer time periods
- if they are willing to give new books a chance (beyond three pages) before abandoning them
- if they are reading more books
- how they distinguish a "really good book" from an "okay" book
- if they appreciate the way an author writes
- if they have favorite authors or favorite genres.

Children understand these questions, and their spiral notebooks soon become filled with Lit Letters that clearly demonstrate their development as experienced readers. The weekly conversations inherently guide them toward the metacognition and reflection that lie at the heart of the portfolio.

For years, children received a single grade in reading comprehension. The teacher, with tests and scores for substantiation, passed sole judgment on how well the students understood what they read. In our portfolio classroom, I don't give children fill-in-the-blank comprehension tests, and I look beyond single scores on standardized tests. Through their Lit Letters, conversations, shared oral reading experiences, book projects, and journal entries, it becomes obvious to me and, more importantly, to the students that they understand what they read.

I am not surprised when most of my students include their spirals filled with their book club Lit Letters in their final showcase portfolios.

Reflecting on Writing: Not a Twice-a-Year Endeavor

By the middle of the year, my students' writing folders are bursting with writing. These pieces were written with red-hot intensity weeks or months earlier. That intensity is sometimes forgotten when piece follows piece and students move on to new projects. I wish I could capture the essence of our conference about particular stories and the students' verbal and insightful oral comments about the history of each piece: why they chose to write a story; what were challenging parts to write; what techniques of writer's craft they experimented with; what revisions they made; and what response they received. Because I know the importance these considerations and reflections play in the portfolio process, I now encourage the children to record their responses during our final conference about stories they have revised and plan to publish.

I demonstrate this process with an example of my own writing. After an oral sharing of something I've written, I share the history of the piece. Working with my students, I have created a "Thinking About My Story" reflection sheet that helps record details and thoughts that might otherwise be forgotten.

Some students complete the sheet independently before the final conference about the piece; others seem to reflect best orally, almost conversationally. They point out particular words, sentences, or passages they like, "tough parts to write," new techniques they experimented with, and revisions they made. As they talk and point, I jot down some of their reflections. Whether the sheet is completed independently or in collaboration with the teacher, it is stapled or clipped to the drafts and published versions of the piece and saved in a cumulative folder. When students read their final drafts aloud, the sharing of their "Thinking About My Story" sheet is often included in a whole-class conference and student-led demonstration of the reflection process. As the children look through their folders to choose their showcase portfolio selections, the "Thinking About My Story" notes take them right back to the conference and the moments of discovery and reflection. From demonstration to conversation to sharing, reflection becomes a regular practice.

Integrating Selection and Reflection: The Introductory Letter to the Portfolio

The first year I used portfolios with my students, I was especially cautious when the time came for selecting the pieces and composing the letters introducing the portfolios. I knew there was a fine line between encouraging students to consider various aspects of what a portfolio might be and prescribing what the portfolios should be. I was especially concerned about those children who appear to be naturally task oriented and who, despite all of my cautions, almost unconsciously infer: "This is what she seems to want, so that is what I will do."

It made sense to start by discussing various professionals who use portfolios in real-life situations. We talked about architects, advertising consultants, artists, and even fashion models. The children caught on right away to the idea that an architect who has designed a wide range of buildings including stores, office buildings, schools, museums, and homes would be foolish to include in his portfolio only photographs and plans of twelve banks he has designed if he hoped to win a contract to design a new, model city. On the other hand, if he hoped to be selected to design a series of new buildings for a major banking corporation, a portfolio featuring banks would be a good idea. Children see that the contents of portfolios can be flexible, depending upon their purposes.

With my fourth and fifth grade students, the purpose of the first portfolio commonly focuses on showing several things: best work; a range of work; revisions, and process pieces; first drafts, second drafts, final drafts, and published books; and often the pieces the student cared about the most. I want my writers and readers to be impressed with themselves, to say, "Wow! When I show you this body of work, there will be no doubt that I am a writer and a reader!" And so we brainstorm together what kinds of selections they might make in putting together the portfolios.

Frequently, I share my own portfolio with the students, and I talk about the reasons behind my selections. I read them my own letter of introduction to the contents I have chosen. Sometimes I show them copies I have made of student portfolios from previous years. I am very careful to share varied portfolios that clearly demonstrate a range of possibilities. Looking at and hearing aloud the introductory letters written by other students makes a powerful statement about ownership.

The children are eager to review the contents of their folders a second time, with purposeful reflection. As they select the pieces for their portfolios, they jot down their reasons for the selections. Finally, they are ready to compose their introductory letters.

Student ownership is encouraged, demonstrated, and celebrated by the teacher. The choices are theirs, but the possibilities have been expanded. The children quickly come to see that there is no single "right way" to put together a portfolio. Their letters reflect their voices, their purpose, and their individual statements of growth:

Dear Reader,

My name is Tamara and I am in sixth grade at Los Nogales School. I enjoy the beach, going shopping, watching TV, reading and writing. I have written MANY stories this year!

The first piece you will read is a description of Tahiti. I haven't been to Tahiti so I had to try to imagine it. I looked at travel books and drew a picture of it. This was the first time I really tried to use focused descriptions and sensory descriptions in my writing.

The next piece is my autobiography. I tried to tell you more than the facts about me. I put in things I like and things I don't like and even the things I hate! I put in some special memories, too. Doing the time-line of my life helped me organize this piece.

The next piece is one of my favorites. I published it into a book. I made up a character called Eek the Squeek. He's a mouse detective. I got the idea from reading a book called Nate the Great. Mysteries are hard to write. You really have to have the plot make sense! You have to have clues that make sense too. I tried to give Eek a personality. I loved doing the illustrations and the cover of the book, too. I tried to write a book little kids would like.

The next story is 'Halloween Night.' I like the dialogue and the description of the setting. I had to work on the plot of this story so I wouldn't give the ending away too soon.

'It's Locked' is another book I published. In this story we were sup-posed to figure out a problem and plan the solution and then write a story. I worked hard on describing the characters and building up to the part where I describe the problem. I tried to make the dialogue sound real and the description of the stuff that went on in class. I think this is one of my best two stories.

'I Can Remember' tells about a shirt I hated wearing. I tried to describe what it looked like, and also why I hated wearing it so much. I think I did a good job as you will see. I HATED that stupid shirt!

'My First Puppy' was hard to write. It is a true story about my puppy. I wanted a dog SO BAD, and when we finally got one, he died after a little while. I tried to tell how much I wanted him and how sad I was when he died.

This year I learned a lot about writing. I learned about focused descriptions, using five sense descriptions, show not tell, specific verbs and not using the same words over and over. When you read my sto-ries you will see that I experimented with different kinds of leads and dialogue. I learned to put feelings in my stories. That was maybe most important. Anyway, I wrote A LOT, but these are the BEST that I want you to read.

Sincerely,
Tamara

Book cover by Wendy Terada

Taking My Turn: Portfolios to Be Passed On

During the last week of school, the final, student-selected showcase portfolios are complete, and they have been shared and celebrated. Sitting on my desk are a portfolio and folder of collected pieces from each of the students in my class. Now it is my turn to add my voice to the story of each child's growth as a reader or writer during the time I spent with them. I review their showcase portfolio, which we discussed together during the final portfolio conference. I also read through the folder containing the pieces that were not chosen by the student. If the receiving teacher in the following grade chooses to participate in this process and has indicated to me what he or she hopes to learn about the new students coming from my class, I consider which pieces might be included in a portfolio to be passed on. I typically make a copy of the student's favorite piece and the letter introducing the portfolio. I look for two or three other pieces that demonstrate the growth or, in some cases, inconsistent development I have observed during the year. I look for the pieces that will tell the story of a child: pieces with voice and personal style. I try to vary the selections to demonstrate the range of writing. I like to include at least one piece of totally unassisted writing. Options vary according to my purposes and, ultimately, the eventual audience of this portfolio.

Finally, I choose one particular piece and quickly summarize my impressions of the student as evidenced in the writing. This is my opportunity to let my voice be heard. At first, the summarizing was difficult and time consuming, but as I became more experienced, I found the words flew from my mind to the computer. I am now able to complete thirty-four summaries in an afternoon. I don't need to analyze numbers or correct final tests; I know these children so well that their stories leap from the pages of their writing. Receiving teachers have commented on how surprisingly accurate even the shortest summaries prove to be. The following examples are written about end-of-the-year fourth grade students. Each summary is attached to a sample that I feel demonstrates the student's strengths at this point of the year:

Marc is a joy and a challenge in many ways. This child is verbally articulate and loves to talk! I am often impressed by the wealth of his general knowledge about a wide range of topics. He listens (rather selectively), but when he is interested, he retains information and small details to an amazing degree. However, his fluency and expressiveness totally break down when it comes to written language. Marc avoids writing. One or two sentences are his limit. He is quite satisfied with pieces of this length and is not really motivated to rethink his pieces. He will add detail at a verbal level, so my main strategy when working with him is to take frequent dictation, help him publish on the computer (a real motivation), and encourage him to share his writing orally with the rest of the class.

This piece is probably an example of Eric at his most fluent and expressive. Eric was new to our school this year and came from a school where his mother reports children had limited experience with writing and where emphasis was placed on correctness, not imagination. He started the year hesitant and reluctant to write more than a sentence or two. Even with prewriting experiences, conferences, discussions with other children, etc., he did not seem to break through to fluency. His basic skills are usually good, but his pieces are so short it is at times difficult to evaluate his editing abilities. He hasn't felt ready to take risks with description and dialogue like most of the others in class.

Just this past month, Eric has demonstrated more motivation, and he has also shown more interest in independent reading. He moved on from the easier Judy Blum books (which he loved and reread) to more challenging books like Indian in the Cupboard *and* On My Honor. *About the same time, he started taking off with our genre studies in writing. The discussions and structures helped him get started and gave him a plan. With this fairy tale, he really worked on developing plot. Interestingly, he has become more verbal in class as well. He loves the computer and is now publishing stories at home. Inserting graphics seems to motivate him to expand short pieces. He is now feeling pleased with himself as a writer.*

Portfolios are not just about checklists, record sheets, and file folders. The preparation for portfolio assessment is much more than a two- or three-day process of review and selection. Preparation begins the first day of school. This type of assessment belongs to the student, yet the teacher has never had a more important, active role in setting in motion the structures that support a portfolio classroom.

When the final day of school is over and I have hugged the last child, locked my cupboards, and taken down the pictures, drawings, projects, and poems, I often find myself caught up in my own reflections. Portfolios, I decide, are a lot like parenthood. When children are ready to leave home, it is tempting to want to tell them how to live their lives. But instead, you bite your tongue and tell yourself you have to trust that the day-by-day life you have lived together, the joy and pain, disappointments and celebrations that are woven into the fabric of your family, have grounded and shaped your children into individuals who are ready to make decisions independently. Likewise, as a teacher, I must trust that the ongoing program that began the first day of school has prepared my students to make decisions about the contents, the reflections, and the self-assessment that are the core of the portfolio. The literary community we have created together is characterized by children who are confident and well prepared to share their strengths, goals, and discoveries about who they are as writers, readers, and, ultimately, individuals.

References

Anthony, R. J. 1991. *Evaluating Literacy.* Portsmouth, NH: Heinemann.

Atwell, Nancie. 1987. *In the Middle: New Understandings About Writing, Reading, and Learning.* Portsmouth, NH: Heinemann-Boynton/Cook.

Calkins, L. M. 1991. *Living Between the Lines.* Portsmouth, NH: Heinemann.

Caplan, R. 1984. *Writers in Training.* Palo Alto, CA: Dale Seymour.

Goodman, K. S., Y. M. Goodman, and W. J. Hood, eds. 1989. *The Whole Language Evaluation Book.* Portsmouth, NH: Heinemann.

Graves, D. H. 1991. *Building a Literate Classroom.* Portsmouth, NH: Heinemann.

Parry, J., and D. Hornsby. 1985. *Write On: A Conference Approach to Writing.* Portsmouth, NH: Heinemann.

Reif, L. 1992. *Seeking Diversity.* Portsmouth, NH: Heinemann.

Smith, F. 1988. *Joining the Literacy Club: Further Essays into Education.* Portsmouth, NH: Heinemann.

Tierney, R. J., M. A. Carter, L. E. Densai. 1991. *Portfolio Assessment in the Reading-Writing Classroom.* Norwood, MA: Christopher-Gordon.

This chapter originally appeared in *Teachers' Voices: Portfolios in the Classroom,* edited by Mary Ann Smith and Miriam Ylvisaker (Berkeley: National Writing Project, 1993).

Breaking the Rules

David Wood

*A California high school teacher shows us what
happens when he substitutes portfolios for the
traditional final exam.*

No matter how hard some of us bludgeon them, certain myths
about high school English instruction refuse to die. These
include the myths that there is a body of material and knowledge to
which all students must be exposed; that grammar instruction outside
the writing process improves student writing; and that final examinations must be given to all students, and particularly the college bound.
If forced, I can make a persuasive case for each of these myths. Each may
have its place in the English curriculum and probably does the student
little harm. Perhaps these myths are insidious only when they become
so entrenched that they are not questioned by us the instructors, when
they are institutionalized by the school, and (God forbid, it must be
coming!) when they are mandated by the state.

Here I want to look at the final exam. At Northgate High School,
a northern California suburban high school that serves a predominantly upper-middle-class, college-bound student body, and where I
have taught for seventeen years, a two-hour final is required in all
classes. Everyone despises them—teachers and students alike. Students
freak out, cram for tests in five or six subjects given over a three-day

period, forget to eat or sleep, and most certainly don't remember much of what they studied for more than forty-eight hours after the tests. For teachers, class management becomes a nightmare, as what takes one student two hours takes another thirty-two minutes on a good day, yet all students are supposed to remain in the room for the entire examination period no matter when they finish the exam. If teachers want to devise a simulation or active participation final, they may have to find a special room so they don't disturb those classes that are taking "serious" exams. Many English teachers have taken to giving multiple-guess or nonwritten finals because they especially dread the aftermath: hours spent reading 150 to 175 essays written on the same or similar topics about which few of the students care, under circumstances that promote bad thinking and writing. Worse, these exams are antithetical to what we try all semester to instill in our students: a love for and careful thought about literature and a respect for all aspects of the writing process. Anxiety runs rampant during final exam time, and most of us, if we choose to think about it at all, cannot justify what we do.

Using Portfolios as Final Exams

So about six years ago, I stopped giving final exams to my senior classes and replaced the exam with a final portfolio. At first, students were skeptical and greeted my idea with more than a few groans, as they felt they had "done" portfolios in each of their previous years in English. That portfolio assignment, which the department requires of all students, consists of each student taking a couple of papers at the end of each year, throwing them into a folder, writing a half page about what the student thinks of himself or herself as a writer, and holding onto it until the end of the next year, when the student repeats the process. Since the assignment does not ask students to think or revise at all, they don't, and, rightfully, they consider it a waste of time. But once I explain that this portfolio is different, that on the one hand it will require thought and revision on their part, but on the other they won't have to study for an English final or take an English final in class, and that they are required to be in class only for the time of their personal interview, the groans stop, and they are more than willing to put effort into the assignment. During the final examination period, I no longer have to worry about either class management or disruptive noise that could bother me or my neighbors. I have also struck a healthy blow against bad writing.

The setup is easy, the justifications varied and obvious. On the last day of the semester each senior turns in a portfolio composed of four papers that the student has worked on throughout the semester. I ask for at least one autobiographical or reflective essay, one interpretive essay, one piece of writing that the student wrote for himself or for a different class or in a previous year, a written critique of each paper, and a cover letter that discusses what the student has discovered about herself as a writer during the semester. The student must submit each paper with all drafts, notes, and comments that led to the final draft. Most of the papers I have seen before and have commented on extensively. I then make an appointment to talk to the student sometime during the final examination schedule for a ten- to fifteen-minute discussion of the work. Between the time I receive the portfolio and the student's scheduled appointment, I read the final draft for any revisions the writer has made and note how the writing has improved. I score each piece of writing on a scale of one to five, based on its overall quality and the quality of the revisions, and I write brief notes to focus my specific evaluations of the portfolio.

Since one of the major goals of this assignment is to encourage the students to discuss and evaluate their own work, I save my comments until the end of the interview. I ask students to discuss what they have submitted, to state what revisions they made and why, and to evaluate their work. I ask them which piece of writing they like best and why, which one gave them the most trouble, and how they might continue to work on it. I ask them what letter grade they would give to their portfolio. I then try my best to shut up, not always an easy task since, like most teachers, I like to hear myself talk, and many students are reluctant to venture any opinions that may conflict with mine. There can be some awkward silences and insipid opening comments, but when students realize that I am not going to let them off the hook, most dig up something to say, usually about what they do not like about their writing. Often I refer them to the cover letter and their own written critique of their work. Here is Laura's comment on what she learned about writing from her revision:

> I still need to work on being more direct in my writing and I can do this by letting my verbs do the work. Often I write something and go back to it a couple of days later and wonder what I was thinking at the time because at that moment I see a much better phrase. Also I feel like I need to be more aggressive. That is the only word that fits what I am trying to say. By aggressive I mean when I read other people's papers they have such power to them that I want to keep reading. My words tend to be weak and flowery. Once again it goes back to verbs. I should really make friends with them.

Though comments this perceptive are any English teacher's dream—and are few and far between—this gets us down to looking at Laura's work on something she has considered important. Written or spoken comments can spark some fairly lively commentary and get the student and me back to looking specifically at what the student has written.

After the student finishes, I make my comments, give my grade and the reasons for it, and together we establish a grade for the portfolio, which constitutes fifty percent of the semester grade. During our appointments, the students also have had to think about their work, and most have taken pride in something they have produced. They have had a voice in the final evaluation and many times have received grades higher than they originally expected. They then surreptitiously leave my class, jumping for joy because they do not have to stay and waste their time, taking care not to get caught by the campus supervisor and be questioned about where they are supposed to be at the time and why they are out of class. For almost all of the students, and for me, it works like a charm.

Reaping the Rewards

Because I reap the rewards of this process and finish the semester feeling good about my students and what they have produced, I do not

mind the extra time it takes me to read and discuss these portfolios—
approximately ten to twelve hours per class. First of all, I get to read a
lot of good—and some downright spectacular—student writing. I have
read poems that were publishable and have smiled through revised
essays that revealed that a student I was sure had not comprehended
one word of Shakespeare was moved by Ophelia's madness. I have seen
what passes for writing in other classes and what students have done to
improve it. I see the writing process at work firsthand, and the assump-
tions on which I base my teaching of writing are validated: that my
comments on their work do make a difference, that students are honest
critics of their own work, that they will revise when it is important to
them, and that their work does improve.

For me personally, one of the most important parts of this assignment is that I get to hear my students talk to me about their work and
try to judge it fairly, which, surprising as it may be to many of our colleagues, they are willing to do, particularly when presented with the
opportunity to do it face-to-face with someone who takes seriously
what they have to say. I have had to put up with precious little postur-
ing and almost no self-aggrandizement. When I have occasionally run
across the student who tries to bluff his way through or disagrees with
my evaluation, I do my best to return to the writing and look at the revisions or the lack of them. I have convinced a few of them that I am
right, and some others have left unhappy, but not many. Good students
know what they have done well, and they will also tell you what they
could have improved and where their weaknesses as a writer still lie.
They tell you when they sloughed off and where they could have
worked harder. Those who do not consider themselves good writers are
many times surprised by the quality of their work when they know they
have something to say and have taken the time to say it well. One student this past year told me that she became comfortable with herself as
a writer when she finally got the right voice in her final draft of her college essay, and another felt that she finally understood how to write a
critical essay after the fourth revision of her paper on *Oedipus Rex*. With
comments like these, I feel justified when I write A or B on the portfolio, and the students feel as if their work has been read and evaluated

fairly when they receive it. Devina, an average English student, commented about her work and the value of the assignment for her:

> *When we were first assigned this portfolio I made the standard reaction any student would: What a waste of time! I did not feel like doing this tedious work on essays that I would be glad never ever have to look at again. I saw the assignment as a snore.*
>
> *I began reading some of my past work. I was amazed at some of the stuff I had written. I was proud of some of the work as well. I had so many ideas on how to change my essays just by skimming over them. I was really surprised. I soon began the process of revising....*
>
> *I think another important thing I noticed was that writing was a constant learning process. Just in the revising I did on my essays this year, I found so much I would like to change. I am sure if I look at the revised versions at the end of the school year I will have even more revisions. An essay is never done....*
>
> *I am glad I did this assignment because it gives me a whole new perspective about what kind of writer I am. I am still and probably never will be satisfied with my writing, but looking back on my progress as a writer sure makes me feel a hell of a lot better.*

Though I have never been called into the principal's office to answer why my students are not in class during the final examination time, and though I have never been asked to justify why my senior grades are higher than many other members of the English department—some classes have received as many as thirty to forty percent A's—I have the lurking fear that I will someday be called on the professional carpet for not abiding by the established rules and that I will be told that I must give my students a traditional in-class final examination. I hope I have the fortitude to refuse. I would like to arrive at the office pushing a shopping cart filled with student portfolios, highlighting what quality student work can be and how it got to be what it is. I would like to be armed with three years of student evaluations showing that students prefer this type of final by about nine to one, that the average student spent at least four to five hours' work on the *final* preparation of this portfolio (many put in as much as ten to fifteen hours), not to mention all the previous work that went into the original writings. I would like to show at least five comments from students who felt it was the most valuable final they had ever had in an English class. I would like to say that, because I took the time to read good writing that matters to students and talk to them about it, I now know my students and their work better, that now we can talk to each other and trust each other more, that the day-to-day life in the classroom is more rewarding. I would like to ask if in fact all of this is not more important than a two-hour final.

I believe the high school English class is built on paradox. In an environment controlled by rules and boundaries, we study literature that we regard as great because it breaks the rules and tests the boundaries. In an environment that compels teenagers to conform, English teachers ask them to individuate, to express themselves, to test their boundaries and find their own voices. Then many times we test them on rules and concepts that to them seem arbitrary and material that feels irrelevant and defies their voices and their intuitions. A portfolio final works because it is honest, it promotes good thinking and writing, and it allows students and teachers to talk to each other in authentic voices. It can be fun. We can ask little more than that.

Bellringers

Mary Kay Deen

This Mississippi teacher of children ages six through ten discusses the history of portfolios, now the "centerpiece in a program designed to record each child's learning and individuality." She argues that portfolios empower children's learning.

I am a thirty-five-year veteran teacher who almost left teaching ten years ago. The numbers of children who were "failing" simply because they could not grow according to the prescribed timetable discouraged me. I came to teaching with the core belief that children need to be treated with dignity and respect. I could not reconcile this principle with new and startlingly negative ways of thinking. Increasingly, it seemed, teachers were being asked to examine children's learning solely for its deficits, to grade and categorize individuals so that at the earliest age possible, some children felt less worthy. I could not be one of these teachers. As a result, I felt I had no alternative but to leave.

I am, however, still here. That's because something close to a miracle happened. A new principal, Kim Stasny, arrived at North Bay Elementary School in Bay St. Louis, Mississippi, and together we traded in the elements that programmed and limited our students for methods that elevated them and their families.

I now teach in a multigrade primary class of children ranging in ages from six to ten. My children, their families, and I spend three years together sharing our lives. Every child's learning and uniqueness is recorded in a student-generated portfolio; the child's family contributes a parent observation journal; and I keep a teacher documentation folder for each child.

My purpose for keeping portfolios is to hear the song of each child. Why this purpose? Rachel Carson, mother of the modern environmental movement, listened to crickets sing and named one Fairy Bellringer because of its sweet distinct voice. She actually never saw this creature, but she knew it nevertheless. In the same way, I intend to listen carefully to and for each child—each one a Fairy Bellringer, an individual who must not be crushed by artificial time lines or rankings. I have no soft set of expectations. I intend to give children an education centered upon justice and community, one that models respect and dignity. Every child will leave my classroom with his or her spirit intact. No child will be limited because of standardization or controlled by competition.

In the same breath, I want to give credit to my small Mississippi school district, which includes just two kindergarten-through-third-grade schools and which respects traditional notions in the community about what makes for a good education. We are committed together to letting our children learn in a developmentally appropriate way and to spiritual and ethical living. Using portfolios is part of that commitment.

Cathryn

If my goal were to "teach to a test," I would not know the special things about seven-year-old Cathryn that have allowed me to help her learn. In response to reading a biography of Laura Ingalls Wilder in which Wilder describes some "bumps" in her life, I asked Cathryn and her classmates to think about a bump in their lives and draw a picture of that memory.

Here's what Cathryn wrote:

It all started when J.K. was in the hospital and we went to see him
Then when we got home we played some more and went to bed. The

*next morning dad called me christine and sarah to his room so we
went and dad said when Mime was in the hospital J.K. told the doctor
I am ready and Mime was holding his hand. he slowly closed his eyes.
On Saturday we went to his funeral. I wore my pretty ester dress. I did
not cry on the outside but I did cry on the inside. It was real sad when
I saw it was true. I wanted to cry on the outside because everyone else
was. When I think of him I cry. He had hart sergry that's how he was in
the hospital. He died of age. We think he wood of died anyway.*

This is a strong and moving piece because Cathryn cares about what
she is writing. In her portfolio reflection she noted, "I picked this piece
because it tells a lot about me and my family. . . I had a bump in my life
like Laura and somebody died in my bump. . . ."

Cathryn's parents responded to her in the "Portfolio Kind Compliments Journal," the small journal in which folks who read the portfolio
can write the child a response.

*Cathryn, I was touched by your writing about J. K.'s death. You shared
very good details from your memory and shared personal feelings
which are so very important. At my grandfather's funeral, when I was
young, I remember my cousins crying and I too was unable to cry on
the outside, but I was crying on the inside.* —I love you, Mama.

*The writing about J. K. really means a lot to me. I'm very proud you can
express your emotions. You truly have a "Golden Heart" that always
feels for others. Learning to express how you feel is a gift. You will
always do well in sharing your feelings.* —Love, Dad

Notably missing from these parental responses is any mention of
errors in usage. The portfolio, as we understood it in our community,
transcended a single piece of student writing. So we could give un-
abashed praise to the content of Cathyrn's piece without suspecting that
this was the whole of her learning or that the mechanics of language
were unimportant.

Lizzie

Another seven-year-old, Lizzie, spent over two weeks prewriting, drafting, and revising her "I am" poem. Her processes included making notes, writing journal entries, and writing trial-and-error poems, none of which would have been possible in a standardized test situation. As this first stanza shows, Lizzie, young as she is, takes command of her poem.

> *I am Lizzie a child, a friend, a sister, a writer, and a reader.*
> *I wonder how many countries there are on the Earth*
> *And when it will snow in Mississippi?*
> *I hear a bird telling a squirrel, "Don't eat my food," and*
> *An owl howling in the night.*
> *I see a bird getting some food for its babies and flying to its nest.*
> *I want to see my cousin, Chelsiea more often and*
> *To climb a mountain with my dad.*
> *I am Lizzie a child, a friend, a sister, a writer, and a reader.*

Her reflection is evidence that the time and support Lizzie received for this effort were not wasted:

> *I want this piece in my portfolio because I want to show my mom what I told about my family. The other people [in her response group] liked a lot of my frazes. I feel I'm a professional writer and typer. I edited for capitalization. I like I am poems because you get to write about yourself away from school. At first I did not know how. But this time I did. Last year I did not because I was in first grade. I learned that sometimes you can use your imagination.*

From Lizzie's comments, we can see what she learned and accomplished. She reaffirmed the importance of writing for an audience (her mother); she practiced working with others to critique her work; she attended to her capitalization; she came to understand that her life outside of school has many dimensions that are appropriate and interesting topics for school writing; she came to appreciate that although she is working from factual material, it is fitting and even desirable to use a little imagination.

Equally important, Lizze's portfolio reflection tells us why this work is important to her and demonstrates that she recognizes her own growth as a writer. Her "song" is of a person and writer, someone we might not know were she forced to condense her learning to a single session on a standardized test.

Helen

As a class, we read *When I Am Old with You* (Johnson 1990), the story of a child and grandfather sharing special time, after which six-year-old Helen explored her own memories of a family event. She wrote:

In my world of wonderful relatives I go scooping with my grandpa. We catch fish and we let the fish go. We don't want them to die because we love them. When we go fishing in his pond my grandpa says, "Don't catch a big fish." I answer, "OK Grandpa I won't catch a big fish." But sometimes I do catch a big one.

Later when Helen selected this piece for her portfolio, she provided revealing commentary:

I want it in my portfolio because I am working hard on my world of relatives. The thing that I have done is revising by adding what my grandpa said when about to catch a fish. I edited my writing by making the first word in a sentence capital correct spelling words.

Certainly, this kind of reflective thinking comes about gradually and requires many class or individual conversations about how stories change as we respond to one another's work. It's the portfolio, however, that lets me see if the child understands such processes as revision and can revise with intention. In the portfolio, a child's voice is heard in the story and again in the reflection.

Sam

I keep thinking about ways to help students articulate what they have learned, particularly about the complex processes of revision and editing.

I am tempted sometimes to give students more direction, more orderly options for their reflections. The case of Sam demonstrates how my good intentions can go wrong.

Here is the original reflection that seven-year-old Sam wrote to accompany his "I am" poem:

> I want my I Am poem in my portfolio because it feels good to read it. It takes alot of work to do an I am poem. I think "I touch the ice of the cold winter wind" is one of the best lines. I Am poems are very hard to do when you have alot of work to do. It was not hard for me because I'v don one befor. The first one I did was last year. Last year I was a first grader. We had groups on one. My group did it on halks it was very good. Vers 1 was the werst it had the most problems. Vers 2 did't Have a lot of problems.

In this reflection, Sam recognized that good work is not necessarily easy to do. He identified a great line, acknowledged the value of group work, and singled out the most successful verse in his poem. After reading his reflection, I gave Sam my thinking guide and asked him to respond again. I was after his commentary on why and how he revised and edited his work.

Instead, here is what I got from Sam when he used my form:

Why did I write this piece? What is it about?
　To talk about yourself what you do.

What did I do once my draft was written? Explain.
　I got in a group and read it to them

What did I rework? What are some ways I revised?
　All of the I ams. switched some sentences around.

I've learned from responses like Sam's that in a classroom that values honest self-evaluation, teacher-developed guiding questions often get in the way and create robotic writing that says little. Sam reminded me to stand fast in my commitment to honor the child and his ideas, to value his spirit, and to celebrate his voice. My "thinking" guide yielded only short answers, a far cry from the joyful, candid reflection Sam wrote without it.

Lessons from Bellringers

If we remember that we teach individuals, each with his or her own "bell," we will cease to honor schooling that stands between the child and that child's potential. We will chisel away anything that discourages thinking. We will insist that learning occurs when children have choices, when they are taught to assess their own work, when they build community with others, and when they stretch themselves, believing that they can do the impossible. Just as the cricket with a distinct voice was known to Rachel Carson, the unique song of each child is known through that child's portfolio.

References

Johnson, Angela. 1990. *When I Am Old with You.* New York: Orchard
Books.

Writing History: Portfolios, Student Perspective, and Historical Understanding

Stan Pesick

A social studies teacher and district consultant discusses his use of portfolios in his history classroom. Portfolios helped him depart from traditional history teaching and move toward helping students think and write as historians.

Too much of the student writing I encountered during my years as a history teacher at Skyline High School in Oakland, California, looked like this:

The reason that African Americans lost their civil rights and did not regain them until the 1960s was because of how Gerrymandering stopped them and it also had to do with what happened when the Ku Klux Klan terrorized them after the Union troops did not protect them and also the poll tax helped.

This writing was, at best, textbook or encyclopedia material rearranged and paraphrased in often ungrammatical sentences. At worst, it was simply material copied word for word. Many students had little understanding of what they had written, and even when the words were correctly copied, students had little incentive to remember what they had transcribed.

That I had to read and comment on this writing made this situation even worse. What could I say? I have no doubt that many students worked hard on their assignments, but in the end, they really didn't care about the words they were writing down. Some students even asked me, as they prepared to write, "Do you want this in my own words?" It was a frustrating situation for both teacher and students. The student writing was not at all like the historical writing that I enjoyed and hoped my students would learn to appreciate and create.

These were discouraging moments, but they started me thinking about the possibility of developing lessons and activities that might move students to write pieces they would want to keep and even read again with appreciation and insight. I began taking steps toward what was to become the "history portfolio" project.

An article published in *American Heritage* magazine influenced me as I moved along this path. The magazine had asked a number of working historians to write about the one event in American history they would like to have witnessed. At what event would they have wanted to be a "fly on a wall"? The responses included in the article were engaging, moving, thoughtful, and personal. The passage below provides an example.

Emancipation

The incident that I would have witnessed is that described in Thomas Wentworth Higginson's Army Life in a Black Regiment. *He writes of a ceremony in South Carolina on January 1, 1863, celebrating the coming into effect of the Emancipation Proclamation. The ceremony was conventional and simple until Higginson got up to speak and waved the American flag before the audience of black soldiers, white civilians and officers, and a large number of slaves, who at the moment were legally receiving their freedom for the first time. As the flag was being waved, Higginson tells us, "there arose . . . a strong male voice (but rather cracked and elderly), into which two women's voices instantly blended, singing as if by an impulse that could no more be repressed than the*

morning note of the song sparrow, 'My Country, 'tis of thee, Sweet land
of Liberty, of thee I sing!'

The ceremony ended as the former slaves sang on, irrepressibly,
through verse and verse. Higginson motioned the few whites who
began to join in to be silent. The moment, as he said, was electric.
"Nothing could be more wonderfully unconscious; art could not have
dreamt of a tribute to the day of jubilee that should be so affecting;
history will not believe it. . . . " This incident epitomizes the most pro-
found moment in America's social history: that point when millions
ceased to be slaves in the home of the free and set in motion the his-
toric challenge that white America make real its own vision.

—Carl N. Degler, historian

This passage illustrates many elements of historical thinking and
writing that have led me personally to become fascinated by the subject
of history: narrative, description, analysis, and interpretation. Of course,
I did not expect my students to write with the knowledge and insight of
Carl Degler. I did, however, want them to begin with the request the
magazine's editor had posed to Degler and the other writers. The
request—"tell us about one event in American history you would like to
have witnessed"—directs the writer to be selective and to have a point
of view. It guides the writer to a key question in historical inquiry: what
makes a particular event or individual historically significant? In this
regard the historian Mauricio Tennero is helpful. Tennero distinguishes
between "history" and "the past." The past, Tennero says, is everything
that has happened. History, on the other hand, is shaped when students
or historians look at the past and *consciously* choose to study or discuss
events, individuals, and groups they believe to have historical significance. Herein lay the first problem: my students were making few conscious choices.

Selecting from the Past

I knew that students arrived in my class with many fragments of historical knowledge gathered from previous classes, family stories, and

accounts of the past in popular culture. I speculated that one way for students to build a personal connection to the past would be to put this information and misinformation to use. Students could revise, refine, and supplement what they already knew. I reasoned that they would be able to do this if I allowed them more room to explore and write about their initial responses to historical events and individuals. I began to encourage—actually require—students to write about what they found interesting and significant from the textbook and other sources and to jot down questions about what troubled and confused them. In one core assignment, they chose an illustration (a painting, photo, cartoon), described what they saw, explained why it was used to illustrate the reading, and told why it interested them. These departures from "traditional" history teaching—a curriculum whose content and instruction were determined by the textbook—were, I believe, a first step toward helping students begin to think historically.

But now I had another problem. My students and I were moving off automatic pilot. Before this breakthrough, I had evaluated students on the basis of how they did on information tests, how much work they handed in, and how clearly they expressed themselves in written work that had consisted mainly of restating what I had told them or what they had read. Although I was finding ways to encourage historical thinking, I had not found a satisfactory way to assess what was actually occurring in my classes.

Compiling a Portfolio

Then I learned about portfolios, a device my colleagues in other disciplines were using to encourage students to think for themselves and to reflect on their work. Simply put, a portfolio consists of selections of work that a student has chosen and evaluated as his or her best work.

During the next school year, my U.S. history students collected all of their writing in a folder kept in the classroom. The papers in the folder were, for each student, an evolving record of what he or she had thought and written about U.S. history over this time period. This collection allowed students to see what they knew before and compare it to what they knew later. The writings in my history class thus became primary source documents, providing each student with a record of his or her historical thinking that could be revisited and analyzed. Each portfolio provided a documented history of that student's understanding of history.

The contents of each student's portfolio consisted of selections from previous assignments that semester (see box), a letter to the principal commenting on the selections, and responses to a series of quotes from historians offering a framework for discussing history and the work of historians.

I want to discuss the portfolios of four students who wrote in the spirit of these assignments. They were willing to try to make sense of the material they were studying through selection of important individuals and events, interpretation, personal judgments, and reflections. These were, by no means, the only students who grew in this way; rather, they are representative of students who made an honest effort to reflect on their study. Brian, May, Mandy, and Clarence used the opportunity to revisit their work, to tentatively explore philosophies of history, to develop historical themes, and to try and use history to better understand their own experiences.

Portfolio Assignment Part I

Select from all the writing you have done this semester:

1. A thoughtful reaction to an individual or event that caught your attention, explaining why you would like to study this subject further.
2. One quote that you selected and wrote about that holds particular meaning and interest for you. Include the quote and your comments.
3. Your best piece of writing on a particular picture or painting.
4. Your choice of a piece of your writing on an issue that best illustrates your work as a historian.

Reacting to History

In responding to the first part of the portfolio assignment, a thoughtful reaction written in response to an individual or event that had caught their attention, students moved beyond mere interest. At least by implication, they began to consider issues of significance.

Brian Keeps His Distance

Of the four writers, Brian is the most detached and analytical.

"The Battle of Bull Run" or "The Battle of Manasas" depending which part of the country you were in. Both the Union and Confederates were expecting a short war lasting a few months with one big battle to decide the winner. There were some people like General Sherman who knew the war wouldn't last a few months, but a few years. The public ignored him. On July 21, 1861 the two armies met at Manasas, the Union army was called the army of the Potomac and the Confederate army was called the army of Northern Virginia. The north was so confident of victory, that on lookers from Washington D.C. came to see the battle. The confederates were outnumbered 2 to 1, but managed to hold on till reinforcements arrived, then counterattacked, confusing the union army, and winning the first battle of the war. This victory also boosted the South's moral knowing they could defeat the North in battle. By now both sides knew it would be a long war.

Brian's choice of the Battle of Bull Run is based on his understanding that, as a result of this battle, "both sides knew it would be a long war." Because Brian is a Civil War buff, he applies the criteria many other students of military history apply: the outcome of a significant battle affects the course and the outcome of a war, and (although Brian doesn't say so) the outcome of a war affects the direction of history. Brian's interpretation of the battle does not go beyond the interpretations in the texts that we had available. His choice for his portfolio seems to be less a personal investment than an example of the clear writing of which he was capable.

Mandy Discovers a Hero

Mandy's writing is not nearly as detached.

Ida B. Wells: I admired the courage and spirit of Ida B. Wells when she didn't get out of her chair which she was told to by a white man. My reactions were "you go girl!" I had to say that because there's hardly any 4½ feet tall female could stand up for herself back in those days. Even today in America many foreigners give up their dreams and live under people's shoes. Wells was little but she became one of the famous leaders against lynching and stop the murdering of blacks by whites. The years gone by, she became a full time writer and expressed the bitter feelings inside of her about racism. She fought many ways to lead African Americans to a better condition of life.

Mandy's admiring comments on Ida B. Wells illustrate her effort to understand times quite different from her own ("hardly any 4 ½ feet tall female could stand up for herself back in those days"), to demonstrate empathy ("you go girl"), and to link past and present ("Even today many foreigners give up their dreams"). The portfolio assignment has given Mandy a chance to revisit her writings on various individuals and choose one who has particularly affected her.

Clarence Thinks Twice

Some students use the portfolio as a chance to revise an earlier view. Clarence says little, in his original reaction, about the event he chose, the Louisiana Purchase. But after learning about other examples of the "harsh" treatment that minority groups received, he returns to his initial entry and elaborates, arguing that acts of injustice represented a pattern and helped set the stage for further mistreatment.

Original Reaction:
The Louisiana Purchase was essential to United States history. It extended the land of the American territory, although I believe the colonists would have moved westward without it.

Revised Version:

*Although the Louisiana Purchase extended the land of early America,
it was done at the expense of the Indians. In purchasing the territory
no one thought with regard to the Native Americans who could have
cared less what America did. This was also done with regard to the
African people, they were also transported from their homelands
where they peacefully resided. Truthfully, I do not blame the Indians
for retaliating with violence, I certainly would if my home and family
were being threatened.*

*The Americans were not finished at telling them to get off the land,
(which rightfully wasn't theirs to begin with) while transporting them
to other places they kept the Indians in concentration camps where
hundreds of thousands died. Although we have not reached this point
in history, Americans also put Japanese people in concentration camps
during World War I,* [at this point we had not yet studied Japanese
relocation; it's not clear if this was simply a typo or an actual error in
factual knowledge] *they also passed laws keeping Chinese out of this
country. This relentless persecution of other cultures only proves the
harsh nature many Americans used to possess.*

Future Study:

*In the future I would like to study more about how the Indians reacted
to their new settings and future placement on reservations.*

Clarence's original entry was made at the time we studied the Louisiana Purchase. In considering this piece for his portfolio, he now had an
opportunity bring to his analysis information he did not have when he
did his original writing. For Clarence, the Louisiana purchase is significant because it set in motion a chain of events that resulted in mistreatment of the Native Americans.[1]

May Links Then and Now

In her portfolio entry, May revises her original response by ponder-
ing unanswered questions. She contrasts the details of the evacuation of
the Cherokees with her own family situation:

After reading the section, "The Cherokee Solution," I was not only out-
raged but also disgusted by the unthoughtful ways Southern whites
treated the Cherokee because they were hungry to obtain Cherokee
land to grow cotton. It was bad enough that settlers took away land
that didn't belong to them but they went a little further by pushing
off the Cherokees into the desert. The settlers themselves came to the
colonies in search of a new life and to experience the feelings of strik-
ing it rich by owning farms and so on. They all shared experiences of
sufferings of wanting the opportunity to be able to cross the ocean so
they could have what they were deprived of in their own land. Then,
from these experiences, they should be able to stop and compare what
they had gone through and what they were doing with the Indians:
they settled in a new land because they were deprived of what they
wanted and in doing so, the Native Americans were deprived of what
they have. I feel that situations are somewhat the same. If settlers had
thought of that, maybe they would take smaller and easier steps in
their westward expansion.

The situation faced by the Cherokee caught my attention and I
would like to do further study of the tribe because I am very eager to
learn what became of them after their removal. Being an immigrant
from Vietnam, I experienced the hardship of my trail of tears when my
family and I and thousands of my people left our country because of
communism. We found a better life in the United States after we left
our mother land. But what about the Cherokee, did they find a better
life after they left theirs? And what happened to them today? This is
what I would like to learn.

For May, the underlying reason for selecting the Cherokee removal is
her sense that looking at this event allows her to better understand her
own experience. May had lived through her own "trail of tears" when
her family fled the Vietnamese communists. She looks toward the past
for answers to her present situation.

A Portfolio Bonus

Reviewing these students' responses in their portfolios shows an additional bonus that the portfolio provides for a history classroom. During class discussion, students can refer, not just to a single piece of writing on one subject, but to many pieces. Each piece has a different focus, both in its content and its treatment of historical significance. A richness emerges that brings different information and perspectives to discussions, a richness that would be harder to create if all the students were responding to the same text or teacher-created questions.

Thinking About Historical Thinking

I now wanted to pose to students the question that Degler's editor had posed to him: why had they chosen what they had chosen? Reflection of this sort needs to be at the center of the portfolio process. I asked students to write a letter reflecting on the choices they had made for their portfolios, and in this process they began to think about how their ideas had been shaped.

Below are excerpts from four different letters students wrote to our principal in which they took a stab at this question "How do I know what I know?" We start again with Brian, the history buff.

My name is Brian and I'm a student in Mr. Pesick's fifth period U.S. History class. History has always been my favorite subject. This may sound weird, but I enjoy learning and reading about history....

I have selected three pieces from the Civil War period because out of all the time periods I have studied, I enjoyed learning about this the most. Imagine yourself in this time period. The nation is still pretty young and its having its first major internal conflict. This was the slave issue. The states were divided and a person had to choose who to be loyal to, his or her state or his or her nation.

I've been thinking, I can't think of any country in the world that didn't have a civil war. I guess having a civil war is one of the things a country must go through. I think it's a test to see if the country was strong enough to survive....

What is impressive here is that Brian refines and revises his view of history to the point that he is able to construct a theory about the role a civil war might play in a nation's history: "a test to see if the country was strong enough to survive." Because Brian was required to engage in this type of reflection, he was led to move beyond the importance of the Battle of Bull Run to a deeper understanding of the importance of the Civil War and civil wars in general. Obviously, Brian's knowledge of the Civil War is shaped by a knowledge of history that goes beyond what he has learned in my class.

In contrast to Brian, Mandy finds a more personal connection to history. She is a recent immigrant who claims she is not a historian, but it's clear that history has given her a context for reflecting on things that matter to her:

> I've been in Skyline for almost two years. . . . My native culture is back in China, but because I am Chinese [this fact has had] . . . a great impact on my point of view.
>
> History, I believe is worth studying because somehow in the semester I've learned how to live in the present by knowing the past. I never hate what other people do to me because forgiving is a way to free myself. I've picked (for my portfolio entry) the Ku Klux Klan. I figured that blacks might be a little painful studying this particular subject. As a student historian my biggest concern about war is the soldier. They fought and died. I cherish their distribution of blood. They are like a secure wall protecting us from terrors. They build our kingdom. The issue I picked expressed my own religious cultures. Chinese had tough times in the past, but I think we're thankful too because America led us to great wealth and settle in the Gold Mountains. I don't consider myself an historian. My point of views are to hold my own interests and not follow other people's footsteps.

Mandy's statement that one can learn to live in the present by studying the past is intriguing and powerful. As a relatively recent immigrant to the United States, Mandy uses the history she has learned to help her redefine her view of the present. In class she had shown particular sensitivity to the feelings of black students as we studied slavery. This sensitivity stood in contrast to the racial tension that sometimes divides students at our school, a tension that is often apparent between the African American students and the recent immigrants from Asia. Mandy's comment suggests that her added knowledge of history has made the present a more complex place but, at the same time, a more understandable one as she refined her thinking in order to make sense of her experiences.

Unlike Mandy's tentative and elliptical discussion of what she learned, May's analysis is in no way hesitant:

> To be truthful, I used to hate history. I could never understand what I have read because well, it's boring, and I detested answering questions in the back of each chapter. . . . The questions that I (now) have to answer are not facts but rather . . . my personal opinions on what I've read. . . . I am able to be creative and say what I want to say because the answer is not going to be A, B, C, or D. Having the freedom to be creative and say what I believe, the work that I put in my portfolio reflect what I think are to be important. Being an immigrant from a war torn country called Vietnam also reflects much of my writing in this portfolio. . . . As you will see, my reactions to historical events usually deals with freedom. I find freedom important in the past because it effects the present. The following work illustrates who I am. . . . After all, history is . . . the record of what one age finds worthy of note in another. (Jacob Burkhart)

After looking back over her work and choosing selections for her portfolio, May notes that much of her interest relates to her experiences as an immigrant from a "war torn country called Vietnam." She does not link this experience explicitly with her concern with freedom, both as a historical and current issue, but the link is present by implication and is further reinforced by the quote from Burkhart, the Swiss historian (Burkhart 1992, xvii). In using one of the quotes I had provided early on as guidance for our discussions, May shows her ability to relate her own thinking to that of a historian before her.

May's comment about freedom can best be understood in the context of our class activity. I had asked students to respond in writing to the question "What is the meaning of freedom?" We talked about their ideas as we read letters from former slaves discussing what freedom meant to them. We read other historical accounts of how individuals and groups tried to make freedom a reality, and we studied how efforts to achieve freedom had been resisted. All along I asked students to revisit and refine their initial definition based on what they were learning. In this context, May produced the sentence "However, my smile didn't last long because I realized that the word 'freedom' that was given to slaves didn't agree with the way I had personally defined it."

Of the four students, Clarence had the greatest difficulty trying to refine his philosophy of history:

The quote I believe most illustrates my, and most others work, is number four, "History is . . . the record of what one age finds worthy in another." I only write about things that are relevant today. An example of this is the issue of racial diversity. It is a hot topic in today's society and have consequently altered our morals to include acceptance of other cultures. The quote I most disagree with is number two, "Historians ought to be precise, truthful, and quite unprejudiced and neither interest nor fear, hatred nor affection, should cause them to swerve from the path of truth, whose mother is history." Each historian uses his or her own ideals in presenting history or else we wouldn't have so many different versions of history. Historians only write on what interests them, some write on racial issues and some on political issues. This is what makes history special, the different and complex versions allow each student to decide what is true to them on the basis of their morals.

Connecting his view to Burkhart's, Clarence writes, "I only write about things that are relevant today." From his perspective, these are issues connected to racial and cultural diversity. He explicitly challenges the notion that historians can be truthful, precise, and unprejudiced. In his view, "each historian uses his or her own ideals in presenting history or else we wouldn't have so many different versions of history." Following this line of thought leads Clarence to a relativistic sense of historic truth: "the different and complex versions allow each student to decide for themselves what is true to them based on their morals." Clarence hints at the selectivity that comes into play as people weigh the validity of different historical accounts and choose which stories and evidence to discuss. Are different historical perspectives competing truths or different interpretations of the same event? Clarence struggles with this question as he tries to explain and justify his own historical point of view. This portfolio reflection has allowed him to clarify his struggle on paper and allowed me, his teacher, to get a close-up of his historical thinking.

May and Mandy both argue for the idea that what historians choose to study reflects what their own time period finds worthy of note. For both of these recent immigrants, the most noteworthy issues are those connected to freedom and to cultural encounters. Brian, for his part, takes on an authoritative voice when he articulates his philosophy of history. In a part of his letter not quoted above, he identifies with a statement from Cervantes: "Historians ought to be precise, truthful, and quite unprejudiced. . . . "

Remaining Questions

This history portfolio project was designed to promote student thinking and learning by having students revisit writing they had done on specific individuals and events and write reflections on those earlier pieces. I was curious to find out whether students, in selecting for their portfolios writings on self-chosen topics, would produce analysis that comes closer to historical thinking than the formulaic answers they were used to producing. For these four students the answer is a tentative yes. This portfolio project, however, was only our a first attempt to address the questions of historical reflection in this way.

In its present form the portfolio project raises several issues. Portfolios promote choice, and, in a diverse classroom, we may expect that students of different backgrounds will make choices relevant to their concerns. Three of the four students discussed issues of freedom and discrimination. May and Mandy, both immigrants, looked at immigration issues. Clarence, an African American student, discussed issues directly connected to race in each of his excerpts. If we think of these pieces of writing as starting points for discussion, might the chance to choose topics be a way of drawing students into a discussion that is fueled and informed by diverse student perspectives?

When we open up discussion in this way, we also create new responsibilities for teachers. Engaging in this kind of instruction means being willing to accept and even create uncomfortable moments in the classroom. Once students are drawn in, developing and expressing their viewpoints, how can the discussion be structured and informed so that the students don't end up with a historical relativism that suggests all opinions are equally valid if they are based on a personal view? Choice may create interest, but it's important to take advantage of that interest by teaching how to find, weigh, and use evidence to support opinions.

Second, while examples of historical thinking may be found in the portfolios, there is little evidence that the students actually understood that they were thinking historically. Can we speak of students' thinking historically if they are not aware that this is the case? Will they transfer this skill to other situations only if expressly asked to within a specific instructional framework? Can the kind of reflective thought asked for in the portfolios make thinking historically more visible for students?

Finally, what role does instruction play in this endeavor? Each of these students was considered an above-average student. I have no doubt that if they had been asked to answer prepackaged questions they would have completed that work and done it well. For May, however, this level of work was frustrating. She wanted to be "creative and say what I want to say because the answer is not going to be A, B, C, or D." How representative is May? I do not yet know how many students, unlike May, become uneasy when they are no longer able to depend on the trusty end-of-chapter questions as a way of completing history assignments. But I do know that too often students—especially students who are not in honors or advanced-placement classes—are not provided the opportunity to work with the big issues in ways that engage, respect, and encourage their ideas and beliefs.

All of the four students profiled here valued the work they had done during the school year and valued the opportunity to revisit it. Their work represents a kind of embryonic historical thinking and suggests the important role that portfolios can play, since the process of reflecting on one's one prior thinking encourages the development of specific historical thinking skills.

My use of portfolios also suggests the importance of the teacher's role in helping students become engaged in historical thinking. The ideas and questions of the students were their own, but the kind of writing and thinking illustrated in the examples from the student portfolios does not happen on its own. The teacher has to ask for it—encouraging, supporting, and evaluating its development.

End Note

1. Throughout the semester students seemed attracted to situations about which they could make moral judgments and express empathy with those who have been wronged. May, for example, chides European settlers who came to America for opportunity for depriving the Native Americans of their opportunities. Mandy, in writing of Reconstruction, says,

   During this particular period blacks became freed men, and I feel happy for them. Then the minute we are not paying attention, the laws which supported them failed. I think its heartbreaking because the laws could provide rights but couldn't stop discrimination....

   The historian Peter Sexis points out that one element of historical thinking is the ability to step away from decisions of the past, however wrongheaded by our contemporary standards, to understand that these actions were taken in a historical context unlike the present.

   However, as outraged as students are by mistreatment, they do not seem able to bring to their thinking an understanding that people in the past made choices in times quite different from our own. Even so, by making judgments about the stories, students may have come to a better understanding of their own moral standards and how these standards might be applied to and have been formed by history.

References

Burkhart, J. 1992. Quoted in *American Voices*. Glendale, IL: Scott Foresman.

Degler, C. N. 1984. "I Wish I'd Been There." *American Heritage* December.

Seixas, P. 1993. "Historical Understanding Among Adolescents in a Multicultural Setting." *Curriculum Inquiry* 23 (3): 301–27.

Tennero, M. 1991. "Historical Thinking." Inservice for Teachers in the Oakland Unified School District, Oakland, CA.

Biographies

JONI CHANCER has taught students in grades kindergarten through twelfth grade for the past thirty years. She received her undergraduate degree from the University of California, Santa Barbara. She currently teachers fourth grade at Montecito Union School in Santa Barbara, California. In addition, she is a co-director of the South Coast Writing Project and conducts workshops on the teaching of writing, inquiry, and the art and writing connection both nationally and internationally. She is a coauthor of the book *Moon Journals: Writing, Art and Inquiry Through Focused Nature Studies* and has written numerous articles on topics ranging from assessment to poetry. She is a recent recipient of the Fred Hechinger Award for Teacher Research. During the summer, she takes groups of writers and artists to Europe and Mexico, where they write, sketch, and paint in their travel journals.

MARY KAY DEEN is beginning year thirty-six as a teacher of young children. She teaches a first-, second-, third-year multiage class at North Bay Elementary in Bay St. Louis, Mississippi. She received her teaching degree from the University of Mississippi. She has engaged in classroom research, studied with other teachers, and learned from her students that we are all teachers and all learners. She was inducted into the Hall of Master Teachers in Mississippi. In addition, she is a co-director of the Live Oak Writing Project at the University of Southern Mississippi, Gulf Coast. As a teacher-consultant with the South Mississippi Writing Project, the Mississippi Writing/Thinking Institute, and the Live Oak

Writing Project, she has conducted workshops in several states as well as in England and the Netherlands. She and her students participated in the National Writing Project's Rural Voices Radio project, celebrating their personal stories and special place—Mississippi. She enjoys visiting family, sharing good conversation with her daughter, and finding just the right treasures for "Booma's Book of the Month Club," gifts to her grandchildren, Oran and Aidan. Collecting children's books, keeping her journals, being in and of nature, and exploring arts are other enriching activities in her life.

JOHN DORROH has taught high school science in Mississippi and Georgia for twenty-six years. As a teacher-consultant with the MSU Writing/Thinking Project, he and his mentor, Bob Tierney, from Poker Bar, California, collaborated to begin a "WONDER of Science" program almost ten years ago. Through simultaneously working with elementary and secondary science teachers, both are committed to tearing down barriers that often exist between the two groups. Author of more than fifteen articles, book chapters, and fillers for science journals, Dorroh achieved National Board Certification in AYA/Science in 1999. He currently teaches biology and anatomy and physiology at West Point High School in West Point, Mississippi.

JANE JUSKA retired from high school teaching after thirty-five years. She is currently teaching in the teacher preparation program at St. Mary's College, Moraga, California. In addition, she teaches writing at San Quentin State Prison. As a teacher-consultant with the Bay Area Writing Project at the University of California, Berkeley, she has conducted workshops in eight states as well as in Japan and Okinawa. Author of more than twenty articles, she won first prize from Education Writers of America for the best article published in special interest/trade publications. Her favorite award is a plaque that hangs on her kitchen wall and reads "San Quentin State Prison awards Jane Juska the Outstanding Volunteer Service Award."

PATRICIA MCGONEGAL teaches English at Mount Mansfield Union High School in Jericho, Vermont, and is director of the National Writing Project in Vermont. She is a member of the Bread Loaf Rural Teacher Network and is a network leader for the Vermont portfolio assessment system. She has published several chapters and articles on professional development, student learning, and assessment. Married to a former teacher, and the mother of four sons, she notes that all of them are remarkable teachers and learners; two of them are currently working in education.

STAN PESICK taught United States history and American government in Oakland, California, for eighteen years. In 1994, he returned to Stanford University to study and investigate connections among reading, writing, and the study of history. He currently works for the Oakland Unified School District, conducting professional and curriculum development programs in the areas of history education and technology integration. As a consultant for the Bay Area Writing Project at the University of California, Berkeley, he has conducted workshops throughout the Bay Area since 1988.

LISA PIAZZA enters her fourth year of teaching high school English this fall. She received her undergraduate degree at Mills College in Oakland, California, and spent a year in England studying and practicing fiction writing before returning to the Bay Area, where she earned her teaching credential. After three years of teaching ninth-graders, she looks forward this year to teaching creative writing to juniors and seniors. She continues with her own writing.

JUDITH RUHANA recently left teaching language arts at the middle school level to become the chair of the English department of Evanston Township High School in Evanston, Illinois. Her two greatest thrills as a writing teacher were winning the James Moffett Award in 2000 and having the parents of five of her students who won medals in writing send her to the Scholastic Art and Writing Awards in Washington, D.C., in June of 2000. She continues her contact with the Chicago Area Writing Project and has begun to write a novel—as all English teachers are inclined to do—titled *The Bone China Luncheons.*

PAULINE SAHAKIAN taught high school English for thirty years, also serving as department chair and district writing resource teacher. She was named 1994 Fresno County teacher of the year and was a finalist for California teacher of the year. As an eighteen-year teacher-consultant and former associate director with the San Joaquin Valley Writing Project at California State University, Fresno, she has given workshops on teaching writing throughout the valley. Currently, she is the founding director of the UC Merced Writing Project and teaches part-time in the Fresno State School of Education. Her articles have appeared in *Educational Leadership* and the *California Literature Project Journal.* In progress is a college textbook chapter titled "What Our Second Language Students Can Teach Us About Learning" from her study of four high school Hmong boys and their writing development from grades nine to twelve.

MARY ANN SMITH is executive director of the California Writing Project and co-director of the National Writing Project. A former director of the Bay Area Writing Project, she was a member of the first writing project summer institute in 1974, while teaching junior high school English. She has also taught high school English. Author of several articles on the teaching and assessment of writing and on the contributions of National Writing Project teachers, she is co-author, with Sandra Murphy, of *Writing Portfolios: A Bridge from Teaching to Assessment* (Pippin, 1991), and co-editor, with Miriam Ylvisaker, of *Teachers' Voices: Portfolios in the Classroom* (National Writing Project, 1993).

SHERRY SEALE SWAIN lived and learned in a first grade classroom community for twenty years. She maintains her passion for the classroom through her work as director of the Mississippi Writing/Thinking Institute, a statewide network of eight National Writing Project sites. Named a Top Researcher at Mississippi State University, she secures funding and works with teacher experts to design and conduct quality professional development. Author of several articles on teaching and professional development, she revealed the spirit of her classroom in her book, *I Can Write What's on My Mind: Theresa Finds Her Voice* (National Writing Project, 1994). She has recently co-authored a manuscript, *From Communion to Communication,* demonstrating that the multiple paths to literacy originate in the cultural milieu of the environment, and is currently co-authoring an article on transcendent reading, which is based on her classroom work with teachers and students.

DAVID WOOD has been teaching English at Northgate High School in Walnut Creek, California, for seventeen years. As department chair, he has been instrumental in convincing his colleagues of the value of portfolios. A graduate of Yale and the University of Chicago, where he studied under George Hillocks, he is currently president of the Aurora Theatre Company in Berkeley. He is building a house in Umbria, which he hopes will be habitable before he retires. In the meantime, he will continue to make his annual September pilgrimage to the California Association of Teachers of English conference at Asilomar, California, where, each year, like it or not, he writes a poem.

Selected Bibliography

Books and Monographs

Belanoff, P., and M. Dickson, eds. 1991. *Portfolios: Process and Product.* Portsmouth, NH: Heinemann-Boynton/Cook.

Berlak, H., F. M. Newmann, E. Adams, D. A. Archbald, T. Burgess, J. Raven, and T. A. Romberg. 1992. *Toward a New Science of Education Testing and Assessment.* Albany: State University of New York Press.

Calfee, R., and P. Perfumo, eds. 1996. *Writing Portfolios in the Classroom: Policy and Practice, Promise and Peril.* Mahwah, NJ: L. Erlbaum Associates.

Elbow, P. 1986. *Embracing Contraries: Explorations in Learning and Teaching.* New York: Oxford University Press.

Gill, K., ed. 1993. *Process and Portfolios in Writing Instruction.* Urbana, IL: National Council of Teachers of English.

Graves, D., and B. S. Sunstein, eds. 1992. *Portfolio Portraits.* Portsmouth, NH: Heinemann-Boynton/Cook.

Hewitt, G. 1989. *Vermont Portfolio Assessment Project.* Montpelier: Vermont State Department of Education.

Kent, R. 1997. *Room 109: The Promise of a Portfolio Classroom.* Portsmouth, NH: Heinemann-Boynton/Cook.

Lovell, J. H., and B. S. Sunstein, eds. 2000. *The Portfolio Standard: How Students Can Show Us What They Know and Are Able to Do.* Portsmouth, NH: Heinemann.

McClure, R. M., ed. 1997. *Portfolio Practices: Thinking Through the Assessment of Children's Work.* Washington, DC: National Education Association.

Mitchell, R. 1992. *Testing for Learning.* New York: Macmillan Free Press.

Mumme, J. 1990. *Portfolio Assessment in Mathematics.* Santa Barbara: University of California, California Mathematics Project.

Murphy, S., and M. A. Smith. 1991. *Writing Portfolios: A Bridge from Teaching to Assessment.* Markham, Ontario: Pippin Press Limited.

Myers, M., and E. Spalding, eds. 1997. *Exemplar Series Grades 6–8.* Urbana, IL: National Council of Teachers of English.

Shaklee, B., R. Ambrose, N. E. Barbour, and S. J. Hansford. 1997. *Designing and Using Portfolios K–6.* Needham Heights, MA: Allyn & Bacon.

Stenmark, J. K. 1989. *Assessment Alternatives in Mathematics.* Berkeley: University of California, EQUALS, and California Mathematics Council.

Tierney, R. J., M. A. Carter, and L. E. Desai. 1991. *Portfolio Assessment in the Reading-Writing Classroom.* Norwood, MA: Christopher-Gordon.

Yancey, K. B., ed. 1992. *Portfolios in the Writing Classroom.* Urbana, IL: National Council of Teachers of English.

Articles

Adams, D. M., and M. E. Hamm. 1992. "Portfolio Assessment and Social Studies." *Social Education* 56 (2): 103–5.

Arter, J. A., and V. Spandel. 1992. NCME Instructional Module: "Using Portfolios of Student Work in Instruction and Assessment." *Educational Measurement: Issues and Practice* 11 (1): 36–44.

Bingham, A. 1988. "Using Writing Folders to Document Student Progress." *Understanding Writing: Ways of Observing, Learning and Teaching,* 2nd ed., edited by T. Newkirk and N. Atwell, 216–25. Portsmouth, NH: Heinemann-Boynton/Cook.

Calfee, R. 1994. *Ahead to the Past: Assessing Student Achievement in Writing.* Occasional Paper # 39. Berkeley: National Center for the Study of Writing.

Camp, R. 1990. "Thinking Together About Portfolios." *The Quarterly of the National Writing Project* 12 (2): 8–14, 27.

———. 1993. "The Place of Portfolios in Our Changing Views of Writing Assessment." In *Construction Versus Choice in Cognitive Measurement,* edited by R. Bennett and W. Ward. Hillsdale, NJ: Lawrence Erlbaum Associates.

———. In press. "Assessment in the Context of Schools and School Change." *Supporting Student Learning: Roots of Educational Change,* edited by H. Marshall. Norwood, NJ: Ablex.

Collins, A. 1990. "Portfolios for Assessing Student Learning in Science: A New Name for a Familiar Idea?" In *Assessment in the Service of Instruction,* edited by A. B. Champagne, B. E. Lovitts, and B. E. Callinger. Washington, DC: American Association for the Advancement of Science.

Cooper, W., and B. J. Brown. 1992. "Using Portfolios to Empower Student Writers." *English Journal* 81 (2): 40–45.

Educational Testing Service. 1989. "The Student Writer: An Endangered Species?" *Focus 23.* Princeton, NJ: Educational Testing Service.

Erickson, M. 1992. "Developing Student Confidence to Evaluate Writing." *The Quarterly of the National Writing Project* 14: 7–9.

Ferguson, S. 1992. "Zeroing In on Math Abilities." *Learning* 21 (3): 38–41.

Galleher, D. 1987. "Assessment in Context: Toward a National Writing Project Model." *The Quarterly of the National Writing Project* 9 (3): 5–7.

Gearhart, M., J. L. Herman, E. L. Baker, and A. K. Whittaker. 1992. *Writing Portfolios at the Elementary Level: A Study of Methods for*

Writing Assessment. Technical Report no. 337. Los Angeles: University of California, Center for the Study of Evaluation.

Gelfer, J. I., and P. G. Perkins. 1992. "Constructing Student Portfolios: A Process and Product That Fosters Communication with Families." *Day Care Early Education* 20 (2): 9–13.

Gitomer, D. H., S. Grosh, and K. Price. 1992. "Portfolio Culture in Arts Education." *Art Education* 45 (1): 7–15.

Hamm, M., and D. M. Adams. 1991. "Portfolio: It's Not Just for Artists Anymore." *The Science Teacher* 58: 18–21.

Hansen, J. 1992. "Evaluation: 'My Portfolio Shows Who I Am.'" *The Quarterly of the National Writing Project* 14 (1): 5–6, 9.

Hansen, J. 1992. "Literacy Portfolios Emerge." *Reading Teacher* 45 (4): 604–7.

Harp, B. In press. "Classroom Assessment." In *Encyclopedia of English Studies and Language Arts,* edited by A. Purves. Urbana, IL: National Council of Teachers of English.

Herbert, E. A. 1992. "Portfolios Invite Reflection—from Students *and* Staff." *Educational Leadership* 49 (8): 58–61.

Howard, K. 1990. "Making the Writing Portfolio Real." *The Quarterly of the National Writing Project* 12 (2): 4–7, 27.

Jordan, S. In press. "Portfolio Assessment." In *Encyclopedia of English Studies and Language Arts,* edited by A. Purves. Urbana, IL: National Council of Teachers of English.

Kirby, D., and C. Kuykendall. 1991. "Growing Thinkers." *Mind Matters: Teaching for Thinking.* Portsmouth, NH: Heinemann-Boynton/Cook.

Lucas, C. K. 1988. "Toward Ecological Evaluation, Part 1." *The Quarterly of the National Writing Project* 10 (1): 1–2, 12–17.

Lucas, C. K. 1988. "Toward Ecological Evaluation Part 2." *The Quarterly of the National Writing Project* 10 (2): 4–10.

Moss, P. A., J. S. Beck, C. Ebbs, B. Matson, J. Muchmore, D. Steele, C. Taylor, and R. Herter. 1992. "Portfolios, Accountability, and an

Interpretative Approach to Validity." *Educational Measurement: Issues and Practices* 11 (3): 12–21.

Murphy, S., and M. A. Smith. 1990. "Talking About Portfolios." *The Quarterly of the National Writing Project* 12 (2) 13.

Paulson, F. L., P. R. Paulson, and C. A. Meyer. 1991. "What Makes a Portfolio a Portfolio?" *Educational Leadership* 48 (5): 60–63.

Purves, A. In press. "Achievement Testing and Literature." In *Encyclopedia of English Studies and Language Arts,* edited by A. Purves. Urbana, IL: National Council of Teachers of English.

Raines, Peggy A. 1996. "Writing Portfolios: Turning the House into a Home." *English Journal* 85 (1): 41–45.

Rief, L. 1990. "Finding the Value in Evaluation: Self-Assessment in a Middle School Classroom." *Educational Leadership* 47 (6): 24–29.

———. 1992. "Finding the Value in Evaluation: Portfolios." In *Seeking Diversity: Language Arts with Adolescents.* Portsmouth, NH: Heinemann-Boynton/Cook.

Roemer, M., L. M. Schultz, and R. K. Durst. 1991. "Portfolios and the Process of Change." *College Composition and Communication* 42 (4): 455–69.

Simmons, J. 1990. "Portfolios as Large-Scale Assessment." *Language Arts* 67 (3): 262–67.

Smith, M. A. In press. "Assessment and Staff Development." In *Encyclopedia of English Studies and Language Arts,* edited by A. Purves. Urbana, IL: National Council of Teachers of English.

———, and S. Murphy. 1992. "Could You Please Come and Do Portfolio Assessment for Us?" *The Quarterly of the National Writing Project* 14 (1): 14–17.

Swain, S. In press. "How Portfolios Empower Process." In *Workshop 5,* edited by T. Newkirk. Portsmouth, NH: Heinemann.

Taylor, D. 1990. "Teaching Without Testing: Assessing the Complexity of Children's Literacy Learning." *English Education* 22 (1): 4–74.

Tierney, R. In press. "Testing Higher Order Thinking." In *Encyclopedia of English Studies and Language Arts,* edited by A. Purves. Urbana, IL: National Council of Teachers of English.

Valencia, S. 1990. "A Portfolio Approach to Classroom Reading Assessment: The Whys, Whats, and Hows." *The Reading Teacher* 43 (4): 338–40.

Vavrus. L. 1990. "Put Portfolios to the Test." *Instructor* 100 (1): 48–53.

Wiggins, G. 1989a. "Teaching to the (Authentic) Test." *Educational Leadership* 46 (7): 41–47.

———. 1989b. "A True Test: Toward More Authentic and Equitable Assessment." *Phi Delta Kappan* 70 (9): 703–13.

———. 1992. "Creating Tests Worth Taking." *Educational Leadership* 49 (8): 26–33.

Wilcox, B. 1997. "Writing Portfolios: Active vs. Passive." *English Journal* 86 (6): 34–37.

Wolf, D., J. Bixby, J. Glenn III, and H. Gardner. 1991. "To Use Their Minds Well: Investigating New Forms of Student Assessment." *Review of Research in Education* 17: 31–74.

Wolf, D. P. 1987/1988. "Opening Up Assessment." *Educational Leadership* 45 (4): 24–29.

———. 1989. "Portfolio Assessment: Sampling Student Work." *Educational Leadership* 46 (7): 35–39.

———, P. G. LeMahieu, and J. Eresh. 1992. "Good Measure: Assessment as a Tool for Educational Reform." *Educational Leadership* 49 (8): 8–13.

Newsletters

Assessment Matters. California Assessment Collaborative. 730 Harrison Street, San Francisco, CA 94107.

Portfolio Assessment Newsletter. Five Centerpoint Drive, Suite 100, Lake Oswego, OR 97035.